RECORDS RETENTION PROCEDURES

Comments about publications by Donald S. Skupsky

Management Accounting

"The NAA receives as many requests for its bibliography on record retention as for almost any other subject. Now, finally, NAA has in one location an excellent book that will answer every reasonable question on the topic."

Los Angeles Times

"Well written . . . It walks readers through all the steps required to set up a legally accepted record retention program."

Modern Office Technology

*"Destroying company records too soon—or keeping them too long has cost companies millions of dollars in penalties, lost lawsuits, and storage hassles . . . **Recordkeeping Requirements** will help them protect themselves and comply with the law."*

Record Management Quarterly

"A wealth of practical information, legal reference data, suggestions and commentary about subjects which are of vital interest to any small or medium-sized business . . .Unique and valuable."

Bloomsbury Review

"An absolute must for the growing business...crucially important for companies raising money or going public, or anyone else who needs to pay special attention to keeping their financial and legal houses in order."

Library Journal

"Here is a work designed to help managers of small and medium-sized corporations maintain their company records . . . Recommended for business collections."

And more comments from our readers . . .

*"**Legal Requirements for Business Records** already saved the Record Management Department and our attorneys many hours of research time . . . No organization with a records schedule can afford not to buy this book!"*

"Small businesses and large corporations alike will find the answers to plaguing questions about how long to keep business records and when to destroy them. Countless storage rooms, garages, and basements will be freed for more productive use. This book is a must for every library and corporate office in this country . . . a real treasure."

*"**Recordkeeping Requirements** is a landmark work. It is important reading for all organizations to improve their records program and comply with the law, and it is certainly required reading for every manager who thought that records management is an "option."*

RECORDS RETENTION PROCEDURES

Your Guide to Determine
How Long to Keep Your Records and
How to Safely Destroy Them!

Donald S. Skupsky, JD, CRM

Information Requirements Clearinghouse
Denver, Colorado

Information Requirements Clearinghouse
5600 South Quebec Street, Suite 250C
Englewood, Colorado 80111
(303) 721-7500

© 1990, 1991, 1994 Information Requirements Clearinghouse
    Second Printing 1991
    Third Printing 1994

Printed in the United States of America
98 97 96 95 94   6 5 4 3

Library of Congress Catalog Card Number: 90-80533

ISBN 0-929316-03-7

Contents

Preface

Our records have grown out of control. Each year we create or receive mounds of paper records, generate stacks of computer printouts and produce cabinets full of microfilm and other duplicate records. The next year the volume increases even more.

The information explosion has created a records explosion. Some people want to keep everything "forever" in case they are sued. Others don't know what to do with all their records so they keep them "just in case." Still others squander limited staff resources to manage records that nobody has looked at in years. Meanwhile, valueless records occupy valuable space. We can't even find the important information among all the junk.

In today's litigious society, records problems could spell disaster to your organization. Records that could and should have been destroyed in the regular course of business are routinely subpoenaed and introduced in evidence to support the claims of your adversaries. Some adversaries manipulate records and take information out of context to portray misconduct or legal liability. Organizations waste millions of dollars rummaging through valueless records in litigation to support a claim or ultimately to turn the records over to the other party. The legal problems alone may cost your organization much more than even the cost of space, staff, equipment and supplies.

Some people prefer not to destroy records in case they are "needed in the future." Rarely do they take the opportunity to determine whether the records will be needed at all and the cost of keeping them "just in case." Attorneys have traditionally opted to keep records for long periods of time because they could not determine how long the law required them to keep the records in the first place. Many followed the traditional "safe" approach and kept everything forever in case they were sued. Unfortunately, some were sued . . . and some lost!

The process of determining how long to keep records consists both of a methodology and technical records retention information. The *Skupsky Retention Method* represents a departure in methodology from traditional approaches to records retention. My approach encourages complete and accurate legal research and consistent, accurate assignment of retention periods. You assign the same retention periods to all records maintained for the same or similar reasons. The retention period is long enough to assure compliance with the law through a unique method of grouping related legal periods. You identify user retention periods along with the office of record (the location for maintaining the official records) and the retention period for duplicates.

There is an order form for these publications at the back of this book.

I addressed the various issues related to legal retention periods in my previous books *Recordkeeping Requirements* and *Legal Requirements for Business Records*. You should be familiar with at least the content of *Recordkeeping Requirements*. Larger companies, in particular, will need the detailed laws found in *Legal Requirements for Business Records*.

The methodology in this book will help you determine the legal retention periods affecting your records. It will not provide the laws and explanations that answer the technical question "How long do you legally have to keep records?" Look to my other publications for these answers.

This book addresses general records retention procedures. It is my intent to prepare future workbooks covering the unique records retention issues of various industries. The decision to move forward on these projects depends on the success of this book and the interest of those working in specific industries. Please provide us with your comments so that we can better serve your needs.

The *Skupsky Retention Method* is not theory. It represents the same approach I have used to design records retention programs for real organizations since 1982. The functional retention method is an offshoot of the functional filing system developed by Robert B. Austin at Chevron in the 1970's and used by Austin & Associates Consultants in the 1980's.

I have substantially enhanced this approach over time. Each successive records retention project has confirmed the appropriateness of this approach. Most clients are surprised that their records retention program can be simple to operate and yet be consistent and accurate. Several have elected to replace cumbersome, traditional records retention schedules, listing thousands of records series, with this approach.

The use of four separate files may seem complex at first. You will soon understand that this approach eliminates redundancy but ensures that necessary information is complete. The basis for any retention period can be shown.

The sample pages presented in the text and the appendices represent the retention method applied to the records listed in Chapter 12 of *Recordkeeping Requirements*. The legal retention periods relate to a small United States company doing business in Texas. Please use this information as a starting point when developing your own records retention schedules.

You will need to customize the information, especially the legal analysis, to meet the unique requirements for your organization. User requirements for records will also vary. You probably maintain records series other than those specified in the examples.

The book uses the term "retention" to mean "records retention." I hope that by eliminating the overuse of the word "records," this book will enjoy a space reduction of its own.

I wish to thank Lorraine, my wife, for her support during this entire project — starting with *Recordkeeping Requirements* and continuing through this book. I also wish to thank Toni Mote, Administrative Associate, for preparing this manuscript and for operating my company so efficiently that I could spend the time completing this project. Finally, I wish to thank Nora F. Goodman, Brooklyn College, for reviewing and proofreading this manuscript.

I also wish to thank my subscribers to *Legal Requirements for Business Records*, customers for *Recordkeeping Requirements* and consulting clients for demonstrating their needs and concerns regarding records retention. It is only through this type of support that we are can develop new products to meet your pressing records retention needs.

Chapter 1   Why Develop a Records Retention Program

Records need to be accessible and convenient for some period after you create them. Afterwards, they begin to lose their value. At some time in the future, you may never need or use them again.

Even if you run your organization efficiently, paper still accumulates in file cabinets, records storage areas, and valuable office space. Hence, you must give special attention to reducing the amount of space used for record storage. Timely destruction of valueless records offers a low-cost solution.

A records retention program provides a "back door" for your records by eliminating the accumulation of valueless records. It also improves your ability to handle important information. By getting rid of the junk, you reduce the chances of filing errors and speed the retrieval of the information needed every day.

Unfortunately, the cost-savings offered by a records retention program or even by records management may not motivate top management to act. Some managers may feel that the records problem will "go away by itself" or that they cannot justify even modest expenditures for such a "minor problem."

The compelling legal reasons for developing an effective records retention program may get their attention. A properly designed and implemented records retention program ensures compliance with relevant laws and protects an organization during litigation, government investigation or audit.

Traditionally, attorneys have advised clients to "keep everything forever in case they were sued." Unfortunately, some were sued . . . and they lost! The concerns related to keeping records too long—coupled with the huge costs of long-term storage—has changed attitudes. Many now follow the emerging philosophy "let's throw away whatever records we can, as soon as we can!"

A properly designed records retention program provides you the opportunity to correctly determine how long you need records for legal purposes and ensure that users have records to do their jobs. The program also ensures that records will be destroyed when they are no longer needed. Records that should exist, will exist! Records that should not exist, will not exist!

Realistically, you have to make a decision. You can no longer decide *whether* to destroy records . . . but only *when* to destroy them. You can no longer close your eyes and hope the problem disappears. Destroying records too early will cause you problems! Keeping records too long could even be worse!

A records retention program offers you many benefits described below while protecting your organization from disaster. The rest of this book shows you how to establish a program to recognize these benefits.

COST SAVINGS

Records accumulating in filing areas, working areas, closets, basements, and inactive storage cost you plenty! A records retention program could save you money in several ways.

Space Savings

You pay for the floor space occupied by your records. If you keep records in primary office space, the space costs could be extremely high. Even if you transfer records to remote records centers, you pay a price — either to manage your own storage space or to use another's space.

Office space used to store valueless records is not available for offices, conference rooms, and other types of productive work areas. Staff may even be cramped into inefficient space. Expansion may be precluded. The resulting loss of productivity could be significant.

The records retention program provides a "back door" for your records. By eliminating valueless records, you can then use the space to accommodate future records or for other productive purposes.

Staff Savings

You waste staff time when you manage valueless records. By destroying valueless records, staff becomes available for other, more productive tasks, such as better managing your valuable records. The savings in staff time is particularly important for those organizations that allocate only a marginal staff for records management.

Equipment Savings

After destroying valueless records, existing equipment can be used again to store future records. An appropriate records retention program will ensure that old, valueless records are removed from the storage equipment and destroyed as new, valuable ones are created or received. You will need new equipment only to replace worn equipment or if the volume of new records exceeds the destruction of old ones.

IMPROVED ACCESS TO VALUABLE INFORMATION

A records retention program also improves the access to valuable information. When you regularly destroy valueless records, current information can be located and retrieved much faster. You can better allocate staff to manage and control the important records, instead of squandering them to manage "junk."

Record users will appreciate the retention program. They can save time and effort locating and reviewing current records, rather than wasting time handling valueless ones. Decisions also will be based on current, rather than outdated, information.

CONSISTENCY OF RECORDS DESTRUCTION

A records retention program establishes the timetable and the procedures for destroying records. Records will be destroyed at the designated time. The program ensures that your organization will not destroy records prematurely. Staff will only destroy records systematically according to organization policy, reducing the chances of inconsistent, reckless or personally-motivated destruction of records.

LEGAL COMPLIANCE

A good records retention program also ensures compliance with the multitude of laws affecting your records. The federal government alone has issued over ten thousand laws affecting records. Although not all these laws apply to your organization, you are responsible for complying with those that do. The fifty states and territories plus some foreign countries have issued laws for records—compounding the problem even more.

See Chapters 4 through 6 for a description of adequate legal research.

The number of records-related laws facing an organization is awesome. How do you know that your organization complies with all the laws affecting your records? Adequate legal research provides the answers.

See also *Legal Requirements for Business Records*, Information Requirements Clearinghouse, Denver, Colorado (1700 pages) for detailed research covering federal and state requirements for records, including the full text of the laws. An inquiry form is available in the back of this book.

A good records retention program includes legal research to determine which records you have to keep and for how long. You can be confident that your records retention program complies with most legal requirements if you perform adequate legal research.

PROTECTION DURING LITIGATION, GOVERNMENT INVESTIGATION OR AUDIT

A good records retention program also protects the organization during litigation, government investigation or audit. The program ensures that designated records exist and that other designated records do not exist.

One attorney relates an embarrassing incident about records subpoenaed by an adversary in litigation. When the judge called upon him to explain why he had not produced the subpoenaed records, he explained in great detail that they had been properly destroyed prior to litigation under the company's records retention program. The other attorney then addressed the court and indicated that he had received copies of the requested records from a former employee of the defendant.

It seems the former employee, upon retirement, took a set of the records to his home. Even though the attorney sincerely believed that the records had been properly destroyed under the records retention program, the program failed to identify some duplicate copies. This proved to be extremely harmful.

Legal counsel and comptrollers often have difficulty locating records in defense of the organization's position. Unfortunately, people often do not know where the records are, how they are organized, or whether they have been destroyed. Searching for the information takes time and money.

A well-managed records retention program helps to identify records potentially needed to support your side of the case as well as those requested by your adversary. The program significantly reduces the time and cost of locating information and helps identify information relevant to the case. You can also be confident that records scheduled for destruction were properly destroyed.

The protection afforded by an effective records retention program not only reduces the cost of litigation, government investigation or audit, but may have a major impact on the outcome.

Chapter 2

The Skupsky Retention Method: An Overview

The "Skupsky Retention Method" includes the same components found in traditional records retention programs. It differs more in the process than the appearance.

THE COMPONENTS OF A RECORDS RETENTION PROGRAM

Records retention programs generally consist of the method for determining retention periods, the records retention schedule and the records retention procedures.

The Method for Determining Retention Periods

The best retention programs incorporate methods for determining legal, user (or operational), or other retention periods for records. Most incomplete or defective records programs only specify one retention period—the total retention.

Legal retention periods represent the period you keep records for legal reasons. User retention periods represent the period record users need records to do their jobs. Other retention periods, such as historical, reflect other values or needs related to records. The total records retention period is the longest of any of these retention periods. Each type of retention period plays an important role in determining the appropriate retention period for your records.

The Records Retention Schedule

The records retention schedule is a report identifying the approved retention period for your organization's records. The schedule identifies the "office of record"— the segment of the organization that maintains the "official" version of the records for the full retention period.

Records Retention Procedures

Organization policies and procedures control the development of records retention periods, preparation of the records retention schedules, and implementation of the program. These procedures ensure that records are maintained for the appropriate periods, meet legal, user and other needs, and are then destroyed.

Legal, tax, records management, executive and department heads review and approve the retention schedule and procedures. Records management then distributes copies of the retention schedule and procedures for implementation.

Recordkeeping Requirements provides details on the content of the program. *Legal Requirements for Business Records* provides details on the laws that affect records retention.

This book details the procedures for determining the retention periods, developing the retention schedule and establishing the retention procedures.

THE TRADITIONAL RETENTION PROGRAM

The traditional records retention approach features a detailed records retention schedule containing hundreds or thousands of entries. You normally determine the retention period for each entry independently.

The traditional approach has the following inherent disadvantages:

- Records retention schedules often identify records by title instead of record series—a group of similar or related records, used or filed as a unit. A typical, traditional retention schedule might contain a listing of over 1,000 records and their associated retention periods.

- Retention periods generally cannot be determined unless you specify the precise record title.

- Similar records may be identified by different titles.

- Retention periods for similar titles may have different retention periods.

- Retention schedules provide information primarily by department and record titles. The retention schedules must be revised each time the organization reorganizes. Since some organizations reorganize quite frequently, the retention schedule may constantly need revision.

- Program development and maintenance is extremely time consuming due to the large number of record titles.

- Assignment of legal citations by record type is time consuming, cumbersome and inaccurate. Even when the preparer attempts to perform legal research, the program cannot adequately display this information.

Some records managers, particularly in the government sector, refer to this traditional type of records retention schedule as a "detailed schedule." Because it is detailed, it is harder to use, less accurate, and more difficult to maintain than our new approach.

THE NEW PHILOSOPHY

The Skupsky Retention Method offers a unique way to organize and apply information to determine the records retention periods. The method is surprisingly simple, but accurate! By relating large numbers of laws and grouping large numbers of records, you can confidently determine the appropriate retention periods for your records. Most traditional approaches to records retention produce inaccurate results. *The Skupsky Retention Method* follows the "80/20 rule" to produce more consistent, accurate results.

The 80/20 rule can be characterized as follows: you will spend about 20% of the time to perform 80% of the work, and the remaining 80% of the time to do the remaining 20% of the work. As a corollary, you will spend about 20% of the time to make something 80% accurate and the remaining 80% of the time to make it the remaining 20% accurate. These estimates of time requirements and accuracy relate extremely well to the new retention concept.

The Skupsky Retention Method eliminates many problems found in traditional retention programs. Because each functional category encompasses a large number of functionally related records in one category, the chances of making errors are extremely small. The new retention program could conceivably be 80% complete and 80% accurate while spending 20% of the time you would spend preparing and updating a traditional retention schedule. The remaining 80% of your time and energy can be spent dealing with specific complex retention issues and carefully considered exceptions.

While organizations strive to make their records retention programs 100% complete and accurate, few even come close. *The Skupsky Retention Method* brings you closer to that goal.

THE FILES

The Skupsky Retention Method uses the interrelationship of four files or reports:

For manual systems, you only produce reports. For automated systems, you produce both data files and reports.

- **The Legal Research Index.** This is a file or report identifying the laws considered for retention purposes and organized by legal group code and subject.

- **The Legal Group File.** This is a file or report that groups or categorizes related laws for retention purposes. Rather than applying many tax laws to your records, for example, you only apply one legal group. The legal group specifies a retention period that reflects the legal retention periods for the laws assigned to the group. You assign each legal group a legal group code.

You assign the appropriate legal group code from the Legal Group File to each retention category. You then transfer the legal retention period for that legal group code to the Records Retention Schedule.

- **The Records Retention Schedule.** This is a file or report that groups related records into categories. Each category reflects either an appropriate grouping of records for retention purposes or a functional activity performed by the organization. Some may view these categories as very large record series. Others refer to the schedule as a "Functional Records Retention Schedule."

Each retention category includes a retention code, description of the records covered; the legal, user, other, and total retention periods; the office of record designation and the retention period for copies.

You assign a retention code from the Records Retention Schedule to each record or record series. You then transfer the retention period for that retention category to the Records Listing.

- **The Records Listing With Retention Periods**. This is a file or report of your records or record series with the related records retention periods. The report looks like a traditional, detailed retention schedule, but you produce it by a totally different method.

Figure 2-1 shows the interrelationship of these four files or reports that provides the accuracy, simplicity and speed of the *Skupsky Retention Method*. Each report portrays unique information. By grouping legal issues in the Legal Group File and records in the Records Retention Schedule, you reduce errors and increase accuracy. By relating these files or reports you eliminate redundancy and improve consistency.

THE STEP-BY-STEP PROCESS

This book presents seven steps for developing a records retention program:

See Chapter 3 for details.

- **Step 1: The Preliminary Procedures**. Before you can develop the retention schedule, you must first complete the specified preliminary procedures. Obtain appropriate approval and support for the program from at least your chief executive officer, administrative department, tax department and legal department. Then undertake an inventory to determine what records your organization maintains. Finally, determine the structure of your organization, the scope of activities, the states in which you do business, and the agencies that regulate your activities.

See Chapter 4 for details.

- **Step 2: The Legal Research**. Based upon the information obtained during the preliminary procedures, you research the laws that apply to your organization's records. Prepare copies of these laws for both your review and the review by your legal counsel.

Figure 2-1. The Interrelationship of Files and Reports Using The Skupsky Retention Method

XYZ Company — Legal Research Index — Records Retention Program

Jurisdiction	Citation	LRBR Code	Subjects	Legal Group	Legal Period	Records Affected / Agency
TX	TCPRC 16.004	TX 115-0020-00	limitation of actions account, open	ACC000	LA4	
TX	TRCSA 5221b-9	TX 130-0040-00	employment unemployment compensation	ACC000	MAINT	
TX	TTC 111.0041	TX 150-0005-00	tax	ACC000	4	
TX						
TX						
TX						
TX						
TX						
TX						
TX						
TX						
TX						
TX						
TX						
TX						

Accounting / Tax General — XYZ Company — Legal Group File — Records Retention Program

Legal Group	Subject	Description	Legal Requirements	Legal Considerations	Total Legal
ACC000	Accounting / Tax General	Includes tax assessment or specific tax requirements for accounts payable, accounts receivable, etc.	4	6	6
ACC100	Accounting / Tax Capital Acquisitions	Includes depreciation, capital gains and losses, and repairs for capital property	ACT+4	6	ACT+6
BUS000					
BUS120					
CON000					
CON010					
CON200					
EMP000					
EMP100					

Accounting — Accounts Payable/Receivable — XYZ Company — Records Retention Schedule — Records Retention Program

Retention Code	Retention Category Description / Cross Reference	Legal Group	Retention of Official Records — Legal	User	Other	Total	Retention of Copies	Office of Record
ACC1000	Accounting Accounts Payable/Receivable — Records related to payment of financial obligations and receipt of revenues. Includes vouchers, vendor invoices and statements; payroll and payroll deductions;	ACC000	6	3	0	6	MAX1	Accounting
ACC1010								
ACC2000								
ACC9900								

Accounting — Accounts Payable — XYZ Company — Records Listing With Retention Periods — Records Retention Program

Record Series	Record Code	Retention Category	Legal Group	Retention of Official Records — Legal	User	Other	Total	Retention of Copies	Office of Record	Status
Accounting										
Accounts Payable										
accounts payable	ACC-00-01	ACC1000	ACC000	6	3	0	6	MAX1	Accounting	Official
accounts payable invoices	ACC-00-02	ACC1000	ACC000	6	3	0	6	MAX1	Accounting	Official
accounts payable ledgers	ACC-00-03	ACC1010	ACC000	6	10	0	10	MAX1	Accounting	Official
amortization records	ACC-00-04	ACC1000	ACC000	6	3	0	6	MAX1	Accounting	Official
bills	ACC-00-05	ACC1000	ACC000	6	3	0	6	MAX1	Accounting	Official
cash disbursements	ACC-00-06	ACC1000	ACC000	6	3	0	6	MAX1	Accounting	Official
commission statements	ACC-00-07	MIS1000	NONE	0	1	0	1	MAX1	Various	Official
cost accounting records	ACC-00-08	ACC1000	ACC000	6	3	0	6	MAX1	Accounting	Official
cost sheets	ACC-00-09	ACC1000	ACC000	6	3	0	6	MAX1	Accounting	Official
cost statements	ACC-00-10	ACC1000	ACC000	6	3	0	6	MAX1	Accounting	Official
credit card charge slips	ACC-00-11	ACC1000	ACC000	6	3	0	6	MAX1	Accounting	Official
credit card statements	ACC-00-12	ACC1000	ACC000	6	3	0	6	MAX1	Accounting	Official
debit advices	ACC-00-13	ACC1000	ACC000	6	3	0	6	MAX1	Accounting	Official
donations	ACC-00-14	ACC1000	ACC000	6	3	0	6	MAX1	Accounting	Official
expense reports	ACC-00-15	ACC1000	ACC000	6	3	0	6	MAX1	Accounting	Official
invoices	ACC-00-16	ACC1000	ACC000	6	3	0	6	MAX1	Accounting	Official
petty cash records	ACC-00-17	ACC1000	ACC000	6	3	0	6	MAX1	Accounting	Official
property taxes	ACC-00-18	ACC1000	ACC000	6	3	0	6	MAX1	Accounting	Official
purchase requisitions	ACC-00-19	FIN8000	NONE	0	3	0	3	MAX1	Finance	Official
royalty payments	ACC-00-20	ACC1000	ACC000	6	3	0	6	MAX1	Accounting	Official
travel expenses	ACC-00-21	ACC1000	ACC000	6	3	0	6	MAX1	Accounting	Official
unemployment insurance payments	ACC-00-22	ACC1000	ACC000	6	3	0	6	MAX1	Accounting	Official
vouchers	ACC-00-23	ACC1000	ACC000	6	3	0	6	MAX1	Accounting	Official
workers compensation insurance payments	ACC-00-24	ACC1000	ACC000	6	3	0	6	MAX1	Accounting	Official
Accounts Receivable										
accounts receivable	ACC-10-01	ACC1000	ACC000	6	3	0	6	MAX1	Accounting	Official
accounts receivable ledgers	ACC-10-02	ACC1010	ACC000	6	10	0	10	MAX1	Accounting	Official
cash books	ACC-10-03	ACC1010	ACC000	6	10	0	10	MAX1	Accounting	Official

See Chapter 5 for details.

- **Step 3: The Legal Research Index**. You extract key information from the relevant laws in the Legal Research Index. Information from this index is easier to review than the full text of the laws. The information also facilitates the creation of the legal groups.

See Chapter 6 for details.

- **Step 4: The Legal Group File**. You will generally identify hundreds of laws that affect your records retention. Instead of referring to each of these laws individually, assign them to legal groups or categories. Assign all related laws to the same legal group. You then determine a legal retention period to represent each group. Use the legal groups for assigning the legal retention periods to the Records Retention Schedule.

See Chapter 7 for details.

- **Step 5: The Records Retention Schedule**. You can now develop the retention schedule. Identify the functional retention categories that correspond to the record series from the records inventory. Normally, you will need less than 100 categories—50 to 70 may be sufficient. Prepare definitions explaining the types of record series that would be covered by each category.

  Determine the initial user retention periods based upon your knowledge of how people use the records. Record users will later review your retention periods to determine whether they meet their needs. You can determine other retention periods at this time.

  Next assign the appropriate legal group to the functional retention category. You are essentially indicating that records covered by the function retention category are controlled by the laws represented by the legal group. The legal retention period previously determined for the legal group will then become the legal retention period of the functional retention category.

  The total retention category is longest of the legal, user or other retention periods.

  You finally determine which department or office will be responsible for maintaining the official records for this total retention period. All other groups maintain records for the retention period stated for copies.

See Chapter 8 for details.

- **Step 6: The Records Listing With Retention Periods**. You now assign one of these functional retention categories from the records retention schedule to each record listed in your inventory. The records retention period for that functional retention category also becomes the records retention period for the record series. You can then produce a complete report of your record series with the appropriate records retention periods.

See Chapter 9 for details.

- **Step 7: The Concluding Procedures**. You now revise the retention files and reports. Develop procedures covering destruction of records, retention of records retention documentation, revision of the retention program, training, and other implementation issues. Distribute copies of the records retention schedules and procedures for review and revision. Prepare the final records retention manual.

  Obtain approval for the entire records retention program from legal counsel, tax, the chief executive officer and other designated individuals.

The remainder of this book helps you to develop the records retention reports and procedures. The chapters and appendices include examples of the files or reports for your convenience.

COMPUTERIZED RETENTION SOFTWARE

You can relate the various files in the *Skupsky Retention Method* manually. But you may find it easier to create a computerized database management program for this purpose.

Chapter 3   The Preliminary Procedures

You now begin the actual process of developing a records retention program for your organization. The preliminary procedures outlined below provide you with the support and authority to develop the program, and the information you need to determine the appropriate records retention periods.

During the preliminary procedures, you will compile information about your organization's activities, products, structure, philosophy, and, of course, records. Armed with the appropriate information you can quickly develop an accurate records retention program. You also can respond confidently and completely to questions and objections.

HOW TO PERFORM THE PRELIMINARY PROCEDURES

☐ Determine the scope and purpose of the program.

☐ Designate who will be responsible for the program.

☐ Prepare a policy statement granting authority and indicating top management support for the program.

☐ Conduct a records inventory to determine record series titles, code, descriptions, status, and office of record information.

☐ Prepare or obtain an organization chart indicating the organization structure the names of responsible individuals.

☐ Determine the scope of your legal research by identifying regulated activities and business locations or jurisdictions.

SCOPE AND PURPOSE

Determine the scope and purpose of your records retention program before you start. Because records include paper, microfilm, computer and other forms of commonly maintained records, develop the program from a broad perspective.

See Chapter 1 for the benefits of a records retention program.

The program provides more efficient access to valuable records and yields significant savings by reducing space, staff and equipment requirements. It also provides protection during litigation, audit and government investigation and ensures compliance with the law.

PROGRAM RESPONSIBILITIES

Some organizations designate a records manager and form a records retention committee composed of people from major departments to coordinate the effort across the organization. Small organizations may designate an administrative manager to direct this effort, preferably someone with records management experience. One person should be authorized to develop and implement the program.

POLICY AND AUTHORITY

Develop a policy statement that recognizes the scope and purpose of the project, designates the person responsible, and authorizes its implementation.

Most people in your organization would rather keep records than destroy them. Expect some opposition while preparing the records retention program. Yet, you best serve your organization by ensuring that records continue to exist for the time users need them, but no longer.

The statement of policy shows that management supports the program and authorizes you to implement it. You need support for the retention program from high ranking executives. When confronted with opposition to the program, you should first try logic or persuasion. If that fails, you can then seek assistance from these executives or exercise the authority that they have granted you.

RECORDS INVENTORY

See Appendix B for a sample listing of records found in a typical organization.

Perform a records inventory for all departments within the organization to ensure that the program covers all major records. The inventory can be as simple as a list of records maintained by each group (for smaller organizations) or a more formal and detailed inventory of each record series (for larger organizations). The degree of detail required depends upon the size of the organization and the amount of staff time available.

Record Series

The inventory preferably should specify record series instead of record titles. You can see the difference in the following examples:

Record Series	Record Title
accounts receivable	XYZ Company Order
contracts	Copier Purchase Contract
invoices	Invoice - XYZ Company
personnel files	John Jones Personnel File
quality control	quality control sheets - 12/89

A record series summarizes the content of many records that you file together, use similarly, or treat the same for records retention purposes. Large organizations may have tens of thousands of record titles, but only a few hundred record series.

You can create record series at the time of the inventory. Instead of writing record titles in the inventory, convert them to record series. You can start with a listing of standard record series and add to that list during the inventory.

Alternatively, record series can be derived from the inventory if the inventory contains many record titles. Similar types of records can be assigned to similar record series. Create new record series categories to accommodate special groups of record titles.

Inventory Information

Collect the following information during the records inventory for the records retention program:

- *Location.* The location—city, office, building—where you maintain the records.

- *Department.* The department or other segment of your organization that maintains the records.

- *Record Series Title.* A name you assign to each record series. Use consistent terminology to identify the hierarchy of the record series:

  Accounting
      Accounts Payable
      Accounts Receivable
      Payroll

  Employment
      Benefits
      Health and Safety
      Personnel Actions

If you do not assign record series codes, you might consider assigning a sequential number for each inventory form and use that same number for the record series code. This will enable you to relate the records to the records inventory.

- *Record Series Code.* A code you have assigned to the record series for filing or retention purposes.

- *Record Series Description.* A brief description describing the scope of the record series, some typical record titles and some exceptions.

- *Office of Record.* An indication whether this department or location maintains the "official" version of this record series.

- *Status.* An indication whether the records are "official" or "copies."

Additional information may be gathered on the records inventory form to determine microfilm, filing, inactive storage, vital records or other records management requirements.

See Chapter 8 for details about the Records Listing With Retention Periods.

After the retention development process, retention periods will be assigned to each record series that you identify in the inventory. You determine the retention period for individual record titles by assigning the records titles to the appropriate record series.

ORGANIZATION STRUCTURE

You need information about your organization structure to prepare the records retention program. Obtain an organization chart or prepare one if none exists. This information will help you determine the activities performed by your organization and accurately identify records in each part of the organization.

SCOPE OF YOUR LEGAL RESEARCH

See Chapter 4 for details about the legal research, Chapter 5 for details about the legal groups and Chapter 6 for details about the functional retention categories.

Your organization must follow the recordkeeping requirements for documenting its activities. The following section helps you identify these regulated activities and the jurisdictions that exercise control. You will need this information to determine the scope of your legal research, prepare the legal groups, and determine the functional retention categories. Figure 3-1 provides a handy checklist for this purpose.

Regulated Activities

The United States federal government, state and local government entities, and other countries have an interest in your organization's activities. Most are primarily interested in collecting taxes. Your accounting, sales, and tax records, for example, are important to these government entities in determining the amount of tax due.

Employment and personnel records are also important to government entities. Government has developed laws to protect employees, ensure the payment of proper wages, protect the health and safety of employees, and eliminate discrimination. While you maintain employment records primarily to better manage your employees, government looks to these records to monitor your activities and enforce compliance with the law.

The third major area of government regulation relates to your specific industry. Some requirements deal with public health and safety, fraudulent or discriminatory business practices, and other concerns for the general welfare such as protecting the public from dangerous products, air and land pollution, and property damage. Government also regulates security exchanges, insurance, mail order, lending, housing, product labeling, foreign trade, foreign currency transactions, and immigration.

Figure 3-1. Scope of Your Legal Research

Use this checklist to assist you in determining the scope of your legal research. Check those areas that are applicable.

1. General Business Activities
- ☐ Business Organization
  - ☐ Corporation
  - ☐ Corporation, Professional
  - ☐ Partnership
  - ☐ Partnership, Limited
  - ☐ Sole Proprietorship
- ☐ Employment/Personnel
- ☐ Tax/Accounting
- ☐ _____

2. Record Locations
- ☐ Country
  - ☐ United States
  - ☐ Canada
  - ☐ _____
- ☐ States/Provinces
  - ☐ _____
  - ☐ _____
  - ☐ _____
  - ☐ _____
- ☐ Local Government
  - ☐ _____
  - ☐ _____

3. Regulatory Agencies
- ☐ Federal
  - ☐ Agriculture
  - ☐ Defense
  - ☐ Energy
    - ☐ Federal Energy Regulatory Com.
  - ☐ Environmental Protection Agency
  - ☐ Federal Deposit and Insurance Corp.
  - ☐ Health and Human Services
  - ☐ Housing and Urban Development
  - ☐ Labor
    - ☐ Employment and Training
    - ☐ Employment Standards
    - ☐ Equal Employment Opportunity
    - ☐ Occupational Safety and Health
    - ☐ Wage and Hour
    - ☐ _____
  - ☐ Securities and Exchange Commission
  - ☐ Small Business Administration

3. Regulatory Agencies (continued)
- ☐ Federal (cont.)
  - ☐ Transportation
  - ☐ Treasury
    - ☐ Alcohol, Tobacco and Firearms
    - ☐ Internal Revenue Service
  - ☐ _____
  - ☐ _____
- ☐ State / Local
  - ☐ Labor
  - ☐ Revenue
  - ☐ _____
  - ☐ _____
  - ☐ _____
- ☐ _____

4. Industry
- ☐ Agriculture
- ☐ Banking
- ☐ Communications
- ☐ Construction
- ☐ Education
- ☐ Health care
- ☐ Manufacturing
- ☐ Petroleum
- ☐ Transportation
- ☐ Utility
- ☐ _____
- ☐ _____

5. Products/Activities
- ☐ _____
- ☐ _____
- ☐ _____

6. Other Regulated Areas
- ☐ Advertising
- ☐ Consumer Protection
- ☐ Environment
  - ☐ Air Pollution
  - ☐ Land/Water Pollution
  - ☐ _____
- ☐ _____
- ☐ _____

The law generally views doing business as a privilege rather than a right. To transact business and exercise other privileges such as employing others, government requires that you follow its rules. Failure to follow these requirements may subject you to fines, penalties, and other adverse consequences, such as losing the privilege of doing business.

To understand the requirements for recordkeeping, it is necessary to determine which of your organization's activities are regulated by government agencies. Start by asking your legal counsel and colleagues for the names of agencies with whom they have contact. You should also review the functions of each department within your organization and the various types of products manufactured and sold.

Business Locations or Jurisdictions

You must comply with the laws in every location or jurisdiction in which you do business. Within the United States, you must follow the requirements of the United States federal government as well as those of each state in which you are legally "doing business."

You are generally doing business in a state if you meet any of the following criteria:

- You have an office in that state,

- You have employees in that state, or

- You have property in that state (even if it is for a short time, such as a truck or railroad car moving through the state).

On the other hand, you probably are not doing business in a state under these conditions or circumstances:

- An independent sales person sells your product in a state, or

- You conduct your business solely by telephone or mail and do not perform any activities that indicate you are "doing business" in the state, other than shipping products into the state by common carrier (U.S. Postal Service, private mail carrier, or private freight company).

Unfortunately, the legal distinction between an "independent contractor" and an employee is not always clear. In its simplest terms, independent contractors are people who perform work according to their own methods, without being subject to the control of an employer except as to the result of the work. For example, sales people may be independent contractors if they sell products for different organizations and contact your organization only for placing orders, servicing orders, resolving problems, obtaining quotes and obtaining sales literature.

Employees, on the other hand, perform services for another person under the condition that the employer has a right to control and direct the employees not only as to the result but also as to the details and means by which the result is accomplished. Whenever sales people sell only your products or are under the direct control of your organization, they are probably employees.

If they have some characteristics of both employees and independent contractors, the law will probably construe them as employees and you will be considered doing business in that state.

See *Recordkeeping Requirements*, **Chapter 8** for additional a discussion on product liability.

Most believe that if you only have contact with a state by telephone, mail, or other common carrier, you are not doing business in that state. You are also not required to collect the state sales tax or keep any sales tax records for that state. In most states, however, the recipient of your products should pay "use tax" for the privilege of using your product within the state without having paid sales tax—but that is their concern and not yours. You may still be liable for injury and damage caused by your product shipped into a state in which you may not technically be "doing business."

Remember, even if you are not doing business in a state, you are still subject to the requirements of the United States federal government for all matters under its control, including employment advertising, product labeling, manufacturing, product testing, taxes, and environmental protection.

Most local governments (county, city, township) do not specify recordkeeping requirements. Many will expect you to pay sales, occupational privilege, and property taxes and maintain records to verify these activities. You should check with the local governments where you are doing business to see if any special recordkeeping requirements exist.

You must also comply with the recordkeeping laws in every country in which you do business. When doing business in Canada, for example, you must comply with the requirements of the Canadian federal government and those for each province in which you do business. Except for some industrialized western countries, most other countries do not have systematic recordkeeping requirements for organizations doing business within their borders. You may be subject to the discretion of local bureaucrats. The host government may request that you produce any record at any time.

Because recordkeeping requirements in international markets may be difficult, if not impossible, to determine, many U. S. organizations develop retention programs designed to comply primarily with U.S. laws. They consider the specific requirements of a foreign country when they can be determined. Consult your attorneys in the foreign countries for additional information on records retention requirements or practices.

Chapter 4　　　The Legal Research

"Statutes" are laws enacted by the United States Congress or state legislatures. "Regulations" are laws prepared by federal or state regulatory agencies under authority granted to them respectively by Congress or the state legislatures.

Once you have determined the scope of your legal responsibilities, you can then embark on legal research for determining the legal retention periods. Legal research involves identifying, analyzing, organizing and reproducing the relevant statutes and regulations affecting your organization. This is sometimes a difficult task due to the structure of the law and the language used.

But non-lawyers too can perform adequate legal research. Legal counsel should always review and approve the research before implementation.

HOW TO PREPARE THE LEGAL RESEARCH

☐ Identify the location of your local law library or legal section of the public library.

☐ Work closely with your legal counsel to determine the scope of the legal research, research strategies, legal philosophies, and other issues related to the legal research.

☐ Review federal statutes and regulations affecting your records.

☐ Review state statutes and regulations affecting your records. Request information from state agencies when the laws are not available.

☐ Review laws from other countries if available.

☐ Use appropriate research services to help your research.

☐ Identify, analyze and interpret the various types of laws that affect records retention.

☐ Perform adequate legal research but understand that you may still not find every relevant law.

☐ Prepare copies of each law if the sources are not readily available to legal counsel or use the text from *Legal Requirements for Business Records*.

☐ Document the procedures you followed to prepare the legal research.

WHERE TO FIND THE LAW

Become familiar with the legal resources available in your community. Many large organizations maintain law libraries that contain most of the source material necessary to perform legal research. Many major public libraries have the basic federal laws and the state laws for your state. You may have to go to a law library for other state laws or other specialized materials.

Feel free to ask your librarian for assistance in finding the material you need. You may also want to review some reference books describing legal research.

WORKING WITH YOUR LEGAL COUNSEL

Legal counsel in only a few organizations perform the legal research for retention purposes. You should therefore expect to do the research yourself or it may never get done! Regardless of who performs the research, work closely with your legal counsel to ensure that the research is complete, well documented, and performed with minimal expenditure of time and money. Legal counsel can be extremely helpful to you in guiding the research, determining the relevance of the statutes and regulations, and interpreting various laws.

Chapter 5 describes the process for developing the Legal Research Index.

If you do the legal research yourself, seek the assistance of legal counsel *before* you implement the results of your legal research in the records retention program. Provide your legal counsel with a complete Legal Research Index of statutes and regulations found during the search and copies of the actual text of those requirements. Legal counsel can then review these in a comprehensive and effective manner.

FEDERAL LAWS AFFECTING RECORDS

You must comply with the federal laws affecting your records and the state laws for each state in which your organization does business. Government and private publications containing federal laws are available in most law libraries because federal law has a nationwide impact. Most records requirements are found in published regulations, although a few appear in statutes. Several sources are suggested below.

Federal Statutes

The U. S. Government Printing Office publishes the *United States Code* (*USC*). This is the official compilation of statutes enacted by Congress. The *United States Code* is republished every six years. Supplements identify new or revised laws in the interim period. As a result, researchers rarely use the *United State Code* and supplements. The indexes are also poor for retention research.

Most researchers for federal statutes use one of two private services: *United States Code Annotated* or *United States Code Service, Lawyers Edition*. Both reference services have advantages over the *United States Code* including: (1) each title is published in one or more separate volumes; (2) the entire set is kept up-to-date by annual cumulative pocket supplements; (3) booklets are issued during the year updating the pocket supplements; (4) more detailed indexing is provided in both the bound volumes and supplements; and (5) each section contains annotations to court decisions that are cited and interpreted. The indexes for the *United States Code Annotated* and the *United States Code Service* contain references to the following terms useful for researching recordkeeping laws: "Records," "Reporting," and "Limitations of Actions."

On the other hand, federal statutes rarely state specific records provisions that affect your records. Some statutes specify only those recordkeeping provisions that apply to federal agencies. Others authorize a federal agency to develop rules and regulations that provide records provisions. You must search for these regulations separately.

Recordkeeping Requirements provides many of the common legal requirements for your records. You may also contact the publisher using the form in the back of this book for more information about the reference looseleaf service *Legal Requirements for Business Records*.

United States Code Annotated, West Publishing Company, St. Paul, Minnesota. *United States Code Service, Lawyers Edition*, Lawyer Cooperative Publishing Company, Rochester, New York.

Federal Regulations

A regulatory agency is a governmental authority, other than a court or other legislative body, that exercises authority over private parties through either adjudication or rule making. After Congress delegates authority to a regulatory agency, the agency implements the intent of Congress through rules and regulations.

Titles for the *Code of Federal Regulations* are revised each year as follows:
  Title 1-16: January 1
  Title 17-27: April 1
  Title 28-41: July 1
  Title 42-50: October 1.

Current federal rules and regulations can be found in two publications: the *Code of Federal Regulations* (*CFR*) and the *Federal Register* (*FR*). The *Code of Federal Regulations* is revised quarterly to reflect changes in regulations (additions, deletions, or modifications) that have occurred during the previous 12 months. The *CFR* is arranged in order of the citations assigned to each agency. For example, regulations issued by the Nuclear Regulatory Commission currently in force may be located in "Title 10–Energy" of the *CFR* and are current through the last revision date.

The *Federal Register* publishes new and proposed rules and regulations, plus notices and other matters each business day. Adopted rules and regulations first appear in the *Federal Register* and then appear in the next *CFR* edition. You must therefore research the current *CFR* and then check the daily *Federal Register* volumes for newer regulations containing recordkeeping provision.

The *Code of Federal Regulations* and the *Federal Register* serve as the primary source of information for locating federal regulations affecting records. The indexes for both services are poor and difficult to use. The *CFR* index has approximately 1600 references to "Reporting and Recordkeeping" provisions. Many references point to a "part" of the *CFR*, requiring the researcher to search page-by-page for the particular records-related provisions. More than half the record provisions contained in the *CFR* cannot be found through the index.

The index for the *Federal Register* is even more difficult to use since it is organized by government agencies. The index does not use terms such as "Records" or "Reporting."You must therefore scan the text of each rule or regulation for the recordkeeping provisions.

Once you complete the basic research using the *CFR* and the *Federal Register*, you must check the *List of CFR Sections Affected*. This is a monthly booklet that indicates the changes made since the last edition of the *CFR* volume.

Request for Information from Federal Agencies

You can request information about records provisions directly from the agencies involved. Some agencies will respond quickly and completely, while others will not be very helpful. First determine which agencies and departments may be responsible for promulgating rules and regulations affecting your organization. Then contact those agencies again that failed to respond or responded incompletely.

Your organization should not request a special "private ruling" from an agency to clarify or establish retention requirements for records. A private ruling is often harmful to an organization and rarely helpful. Most regulatory agencies are very restrictive in private rulings and tend to be more conservative in their approach than necessary. Nothing prevents an organization from interpreting and relying upon the law just as it is written. Once you obtain a private ruling, however, it may bind you but not other organizations. If you contact a regulatory agency, ask only that they tell you "which laws affect the records of your organization."

A few regulatory agencies publish opinions and rulings in other sources. For example, the Internal Revenue Service publishes *Revenue Rulings* and *Revenue Procedures* on a weekly basis. Except for the Internal Revenue Service, you will rarely find a retention provision in one of these other sources.

STATE LAWS AFFECTING RECORDS

State laws affecting records are more difficult to find than federal laws. Sometimes state statutes and regulations are similar to the federal laws. In other cases, the state laws are totally different.

See Chapter 3 for determining in which states you are "doing business."

An organization should review the laws for every state in which it "does business." As a minimum, you should research state statutes and regulations for every state in which your organization has employees, an office or facility, or does a substantial volume of business. Legal research for state law will be substantially more difficult and time consuming than federal research.

State Statutes

You probably will find statutes for your state in local public libraries. State statutes for other states may only exist in law libraries. Some smaller law libraries may maintain statutes only for the home state or for states in the surrounding geographical area.

The amount of records-related provisions found in state statutes varies dramatically from state to state. Some state legislatures will approve and publish statutes containing the rules and regulations prepared by state regulatory agencies. Other states publish these regulations separately.

The quality of the indexes to the state statutes also varies substantially. Check under a variety of indexing terms including "Records" and "Recordkeeping" to find the information you need.

State Regulations

About forty states publish their regulations through state printing offices or private contractors. The other ten states do not publish regulations at all. You must request the regulations directly from the agencies.

You may purchase these regulations and subscribe to updates for those states in which you do business. If your organization conducts business nationwide, the cost of these rules and regulations could exceed $35,000 for the one-time purchase and $10,000 annually for updates.

The Library of Congress, Legal Reading Room (Washington, DC) is probably the only place in the country where you can find published state regulations for several, but not all, states in one location.

The quality of the indexes for state regulations also vary dramatically. Occasionally, index include terms such as "Records and Reporting" to assist the researcher. More often, the indexes fail to include references to recordkeeping provisions. You must then scan the subject matter to locate the relevant information.

Requests for Information from State Agencies

You can request the appropriate state agencies to provide you with copies of the laws. This may be the only way to get state regulations, especially for those states that do not publish them. Many state agencies will actually help you comply with their laws. Some may charge you for copies of the relevant publications. Keep a record of the agencies contacted and the responses received to show that your organization made a good faith attempt to comply with the state law. Ask the agency to respond even if no laws exist. The record of research and procedures followed could be very important if you miss an important law and have to explain the oversight to a government agency.

OTHER RESEARCH SERVICES

You should consider three other sources of information to simplify the research task.

Legal Requirements for Business Records

Legal Requirements for Business Records, Information Requirements Clearinghouse, Denver, Colorado, 1700 pages. Annual update service also available.

Legal Requirements for Business Records is a three-volume looseleaf service dedicated to reporting the laws published by the state and federal governments affecting recordkeeping. The publication contains the full text of the actual laws affecting records, the source citation, a series of comprehensive indexes, and informative articles to help you quickly and confidently locate the laws affecting your records.

The *Federal Requirements* contains the recordkeeping provisions found in federal statutes and regulations for all regulated industries and activities. The *State Requirements* contains the basic state provisions needed by most organizations in the areas of tax, employment, statutes of limitation, business organization and records media.

Legal Requirements for Business Records served as the source for information for this book.

Full Text Data Bases

LEXIS is owned by Mead Data Central, Dayton, Ohio. WESTLAW is owned by West Publishing Company, St. Paul, Minnesota.

LEXIS and WESTLAW are on-line, full text legal information retrieval systems that provide access to federal statutes and regulations plus most state statutes. Only a few state regulations are available through these services.

Both systems enable you to access the full text of the law based on your search inquiries. For example, the inquiry "RECORD OR DOCUMENT OR REPORT W/10 KEEP OR STORE OR RETRIEVE OR MAINTAIN OR RETAIN" will identify laws in the database, such as: "records shall be maintained for three years" but also "documents may be maintained in microfilm form."

Because these databases contain the full text of the entire statute or regulation, rather than just recordkeeping provisions, you will often retrieve laws not relevant to your purposes. You also will have difficulty locating laws that contain inconsistent or unusual terminology that you did not anticipate in the search.

Guide to Records Retention Requirements

Contact Superintendent of Documents, U.S. Government Printing Office, Washington D.C. 20402

The National Archives and Records Administration, through the Office of the Federal Register, publishes the *Guide to Record Retention Requirements* with annual supplements. The *Guide* contains abstracts of many laws affecting records found in the federal statutes and regulations, including retention periods. Information is organized by federal government agency.

While the abstracts may be useful to identify some basic records retention information, they generally do not provide you with the information needed to accurately determine records retention periods. First, the information is not complete even for federal law and by design contains no state law. Second, the index is not complete, so you will have difficulty locating all the laws affecting your industry. Third, you will still have to go to the library and read the full text of the laws to determine their applicability to your records.

TYPES OF LAWS AFFECTING RECORDS

Legal research will uncover the laws affecting the retention of records for legal purposes. Some laws clearly state the legal requirements. If you operate in several states, however, you can encounter different requirements affecting the same records. You must then determine which of these laws to follow.

Other laws that affect your records either do not state a specific retention period or merely give a legal consideration, such as a statute of limitation. These, too, must be considered when developing the records retention program.

This book provides a methodology to identify, organize and evaluate relevant laws in a simple, accurate manner.

Recordkeeping Requirements, **Chapters 6 to 8 also discuss these categories of laws in depth.**

You will encounter five categories of laws that could affect the records retention periods for your records:

- Requirements to keep records that do not state retention periods.

- Requirements to keep records for specified retention periods.

- Statute of limitations or limitations of action periods that specify when legal actions or lawsuits can be initiated.

- Limitation of assessment periods that specify when your taxes may be assessed and tax records audited.

- Pending or imminent litigation, government investigation or audit affecting certain records.

Often several different types of laws will affect the retention periods.

Requirements to Keep Records that Do Not State Retention Periods

See *Recordkeeping Requirements*, Chapter 7 for the detailed legal analysis supporting the "three-year presumption."

Many requirements to keep records do not specify how long they must be kept. In this situation, you need to keep these records only for a "reasonable" period. While the definition of "reasonable" varies according to your perspective, a strong argument can be made that it is always reasonable to keep records for three years if the law does not specify a different retention period.

Illinois, Maryland, New Hampshire, Oklahoma and Texas have adopted laws confirming that records that are required to be kept by state law can be destroyed after three years, unless a specific retention period is stated in the law.

The Paperwork Reduction Act of 1980, statutes in five states, other common records retention periods, and realistic business practices support this three-year presumption. However, this is a "three-year presumption" and not a "three-year fact."

Requirements to Keep Records for Specified Retention Periods

Many laws containing recordkeeping requirements do state a specific retention period. Here is an example from the U.S. Department of Labor regulations implementing the Fair Labor Standards Act:

The United States Department of Labor Wage and Hour Division regulations implementing the Fair Labor Standards Act. 29 CFR § 516.5.

PART 516—RECORDS TO BE KEPT BY EMPLOYERS

§516.5 Records to be preserved 3 years.

Each employer shall preserve for at least three years: (a) *Payroll records*. From the last date of entry, all payroll or other records containing the employee information and data required under any of the applicable sections of this part . . .

The Internal Revenue Service requires employers to maintain records supporting employment taxes for four years. Here is the text of that law:

See United States Internal Revenue Service tax regulations related to employment tax. 26 CFR § 31.6001-1.

PART 31—EMPLOYMENT TAXES AND COLLECTION OF INCOME TAX AT SOURCE

§31.6001-1 Records In General.

(e) *Place and period for keeping records. . .*

(2) Except as otherwise provided in the following sentence, every person required by the regulations in this part to keep records in respect of a tax (whether or not such person incurs liability for such tax) shall maintain such records for at least four years after the due date of such tax for the return period to which the records relate or the date such tax is paid, whichever is the latter . . .

The Department of Labor requires you to keep payroll records for three years while the IRS specifies four years for the same records. When confronted with differing requirements for records retention, generally keep the records for the longest period stated. This ensures that you meet the requirements of every law.

Statute of Limitation or Limitation of Action Periods that Specify When Legal Actions or Law Suits Can Be Initiated

"Statutes of limitation" or "limitations of action" are laws prescribing the time during which a legal action or lawsuit may be initiated. Once the statute of limitations ends, no further legal action can be brought for a specific matter.

Records are often the principal form of evidence used in litigation, either to defend a party's position or to show that the other party acted improperly. Court rules permit parties to subpoena the records of the opposition and use them effectively to pursue their claims.

This is a complicated issue and requires careful consideration. *Recordkeeping Requirements,* Chapter 7 provides detailed strategies and reviews potential pitfalls related to retaining or destroying records before the statute of limitations expires.

While a statute of limitations may relate to matters for which records have an important role, the statute of limitations itself does not require that you keep records. During the period specified by the statute of limitations, you may or may not want to keep records, according to your judgment as to the possibility and severity of adverse claims.

A typical statute of limitations that may impact on the legal retention period for contracts reads as follows:

California Code of Civil Procedure § 337.

CHAPTER 3. THE TIME OF COMMENCING ACTIONS OTHER THAN FOR THE RECOVERY OF REAL PROPERTY

§337. Four years: Written contract . . .

Within four years: 1. An action upon any contract, obligation or liability founded upon an instrument in writing . . .

In California, for example, a court action can be brought within four years of the breach of a contract to compel performance, recover damages, or to collect payments due. While an organization does not have to keep records during the statute of limitations period, you may still want records to defend your claims during litigation.

The courts are emphatic, however, that records should not be destroyed either just before or during litigation with the intent to deprive the other party of relevant information.

Limitation of Assessment Periods That Specify When Your Taxes May Be Assessed and Tax Records Audited

"Limitations of assessment" are similar to statutes of limitation except that they refer to the period that the tax agency can determine the taxes owed. Under most circumstances, if the agency fails to act within the limitation of assessment period, the taxes are the amount stated on your tax return.

The tax agency, on the other hand, has the right to audit your records at any time prior to the termination of the limitation of assessment period (and beyond if you agree to an extension of the limitation of assessment period). Unlike a statute of limitation, if you do not have tax records during this period to support your tax return, you can be fined or penalized, your claims for deductions or your characterization of income may be disallowed, and your taxes calculated according to the tax agency's own formula, rather than your calculations.

Most states require the assessment to be completed within three years after the return was filed or the return was due, whichever is later. A typical provision is found in New York:

See Consolidated Laws of New York, Tax Law, § 1083.

Article 27. Corporate Tax Procedure and Administration.

§1083. Limitations on assessment.

(a) General.—Except as otherwise provided in this section, any tax . . . shall be assessed within three years after the return was filed . . .

Most states have exceptions to this general rule. For example, taxes can be assessed for a six year period if you understate your income by 25 percent or more. This period can be extended indefinitely if you file a false return, fail to file, or agree to extend the assessment period (audit).

Tax records should be kept at least during the basic, minimum limitation of assessment period. You should maintain the records during the exception period if you determine that your organization faces a reasonable risk of audit under one of those exceptions.

Pending or Imminent Litigation, Government Investigation or Audit Affecting Certain Records

Even after you implement the records retention program, you may be required to keep certain records for a longer period because of litigation, government investigation or audit. The courts have consistently concluded that pertinent records must be maintained while these actions are pending or imminent. While most people expect to keep pertinent records while matters are in progress, few realize that they must also keep them while the matters are "imminent"—close to being initiated.

A lawsuit is considered imminent when you have been advised by the other party that a lawsuit will be initiated or have reasons to believe, based upon investigations and overtures, that the other party is preparing or seriously considering the lawsuit. Similarly, a government investigation is imminent when you receive notice that the government will soon investigate your organization.

When litigation or a government investigation or audit is pending or imminent, do not destroy relevant records until the matter is complete. Retain and protect these records until it is clear that they will no longer be needed for these actions. The courts impose severe punishment on people who destroy records in violation of a court order or to deliberately obstruct justice.

You can sometimes obtain permission from the court or government agency to destroy relevant records before the action ends. Otherwise, your legal counsel should identify records that are unrelated to the matter. Most often you will simply have to keep the records until the matter has been completed. Finally, the courts or government agency may require you to maintain the records for some time after the action has concluded as part of the settlement order or in case other similar matters should arise.

WHEN NO LAWS AFFECT RECORDS

Some people mistakenly believe that laws control all records. This is not true. Many records created and used by organizations are not covered by any law—federal, state, or local. Organizations create these "internal" records purely to support the conduct of their business.

When you find that no legal requirements exist for certain records, select the records retention period that best serves the needs of the organization. The actual retention period can, therefore, be as short as a few weeks or months, or extend several years.

Some people, being conservative, still keep these records for three years—treating them the same way as records required to be maintained but for which the law does not give a specific retention period. This practice offers a protective blanket for those situations where a legal requirement may exist but could not be found after adequate legal research.

It would also be reasonable to decide that no legal retention periods apply for these records and keep them only as long as they are needed by the users in your organization. But you

Although some records do not have to be created in the first place, courts have taken the position that these records, as well as required records, should be destroyed only under an approved records retention program.

can safely conclude that no legal periods exist for certain records only after completing adequate legal research.

Granted, some laws are extremely difficult to locate even by an experienced researcher. Failure to conduct adequate legal research, however, is never a valid excuse for not finding records requirements. On the other hand, while "ignorance of the law is no excuse," the inability to find the law after reasonable legal research just may be.

INABILITY TO FIND LAWS AFFECTING RECORDS

You are expected to comply with statutes and regulations. Penalties for failing to comply could include fines and imprisonment. Our system for publishing and indexing the law, however, is not designed for researching laws affecting records. The research process is also made more difficult because it must often be done by people without legal training.

Even the best researcher will not find *all* the legal provisions contained in statutes and regulations. You can usually find many of the more obvious laws by using research methods— such as indexes, computer-assisted research, and visual scanning—but do not expect to find them all.

You must comply with legal requirements that affect your records. You also may comply with legal considerations or choose not to follow them. Chapter 6 provides detailed information on how to distinguish between legal requirements and legal considerations, and how to determine the appropriate records retention periods.

The law is not clear about the potential consequences if you do not find particular statutes or regulations even after exhaustive research. Normally, "ignorance of the law is no excuse" for non-compliance with legal requirements. Fundamental fairness and public policy dictate that it would be blatantly unfair, however, to punish you for not finding some laws after a reasonable research effort, especially since some laws are so difficult to find. You should be cautioned, that this doctrine of "inability to find the law as an excuse" has never been upheld by the courts.

To protect your organization, document the research performed, indicating the methods used, the citations examined, and the requirements found. You could then present the information in an administrative or judicial hearing to explain the conduct of the organization and, perhaps, avoid any adverse consequences arising from the failure to comply with legal requirements.

TEXT OF THE LEGAL RESEARCH

If your legal counsel has access to *Legal Requirements for Business Records*, you do not have to reproduce laws contained in that service. The Legal Research Index described in Chapter 5 contains the citations enabling your legal counsel to quickly find the text.

Whenever you identify a legal requirement, reproduce the relevant pages and highlight the specific paragraphs applicable to your records. Also reproduce the cover page of the publication to indicate the source of the law. Finally, reproduce additional indexes, titles, or subsections to indicate the structure of the law and, perhaps, its applicability to your organization.

Organize your copies of the law according to citation, by jurisdiction (federal or state), and statute or regulation. Legal counsel needs to review the full text of the law. Although, most lawyers do have access to law libraries, the review will proceed much quicker if you provide the text of the law. State regulations in particular may not readily be available.

Chapter 5   The Legal Research Index

You will encounter several federal and state laws that affect your records program. Organize and index this information in the Legal Research Index before using it.

Appendix D shows a sample Legal Research Index for a United States company doing business in one state.

Figure 5-2 shows a sample page from a Legal Research Index. This chapter describes the content and the process for creating and customizing the Legal Research Index to meet the needs of your organization.

HOW TO PREPARE THE LEGAL RESEARCH INDEX

☐ Prepare the legal research.

Use index cards for manual indexes.

☐ Enter the index information including jurisdiction, citation, reference code, subject, legal period, records affected and agency. Prepare multiple entries if a law contains two or more legal periods.

☐ Sort the index entries by subject.

See Chapter 6 for details about the Legal Group File

After you create the Legal Group File, you will insert legal group codes in the Legal Research Index, sort the report again, and prepare the printed report.

ADVANTAGES

You create the Legal Research Index for the following reasons:

- *Future reference.* Organize the legal research so that information can be found quickly. The research can

Figure 5-1. Contents and Abbreviations for the Legal Research Index

CONTENTS

The Legal Research Index in Figure 5-2 contains the following information:

Jurisdiction. The location where the law applies — e.g. state or federal.

Citation. The actual citation to the publication containing the law.

LRBR Code. The 14-digit code used by *Legal Requirements for Business Records* to uniquely identify laws.

Subject. The two- or three-line hierarchical subject or functional classification used to summarize the content of the law.

Legal Group Code. The code used to group related laws. Add entries for laws affecting different legal groups. See Chapter 6 for details for creating the legal group code.

Legal Period. The abbreviation summarizing the legal period affecting records. Add entries for laws containing different legal periods.

Records Affected. The records specified in the law. Many laws do not specify records by name, but identify types of information.

Agency. The agency responsible for administering the law. Some laws are not administered by specific agencies.

ABBREVIATIONS (See Appendix E for details.)

ATX:	ACT+TAX, active plus tax filing date.
AS:	limitation of assessment.
CY:	current year.
D:	days.
LA:	limitation of action.
IND:	indefinite.
MAINT:	maintain.
M:	months.
SL:	statute of limitations.
TAX:	tax filing date.
Y:	years.
number:	period of time
+:	plus.

Express time periods in years, unless the law specifies months or days.

Figure 5-2. Sample Legal Research Index

Jur.	Citation	LRBR Code	Subjects	Legal Group	Legal Period	Records Affected / Agency
US	26 CFR 1.6001-1	US 226-0970-00	tax income	ACC000	IND	accounting records Internal Revenue Service
US	26 CFR 31.6001-1	US 226-1090-00	tax employment	ACC000	4	payroll records Internal Revenue Service
US	26 CFR 31.6001-2	US 226-1100-00	tax employment	ACC000	4	payroll records Internal Revenue Service
US	26 CFR 31.6001-4	US 226-1130-00	tax employment	ACC000	4	payroll records;unemployment taxes Internal Revenue Service
US	26 CFR 31.6001-5	US 226-1150-00	tax employment	ACC000	4	payroll records Internal Revenue Service
US	26 CFR 301.6501(A)-1	US 226-1870-00	tax income - assessment general	ACC000	AS3	accounting records Internal Revenue Service
US	26 CFR 301.6501(C)-1	US 226-1880-00	tax income - assessment fraud	ACC000	ASIND	accounting records Internal Revenue Service
US	26 CFR 301.6501(E)-1	US 226-1890-00	tax gift - assessment understatement by 25%	ACC000	AS6	accounting records Internal Revenue Service
US	26 CFR 301.6501(E)-1	US 226-1890-00	tax income - assessment understatement by 25%	ACC000	AS6	accounting records Internal Revenue Service
US	26 CFR 301.6532-1(A)	US 226-1960-00	tax income - suit	ACC000	LA2	accounting records Internal Revenue Service
US	26 CFR 301.6532-2	US 226-1970-00	tax income - suit	ACC000	LA2	accounting records Internal Revenue Service
US	29 CFR 5.5	US 229-0040-00	contract federal - payroll	ACC000	3	payroll records Labor, Department of
US	29 CFR 516.5	US 229-0300-00	employment payroll records	ACC000	3	payroll records Labor, Department of: Wage and Hour Division
US	29 CFR 1620.22(B)	US 229-0910-00	limitation of actions wages, recovery of	ACC000	LA3	payroll records Equal Employment Opportunity Commission

then be used for developing the records program and for answering questions regarding the laws.

- *Completeness.* By organizing the research and preparing indexes, you can ensure that the research is complete. You can also readily determine the areas in which more research may be necessary.

- *Simplifying the legal analysis.* You will consider many difficult, overlapping, and sometimes contradictory laws when developing the records retention program. An index helps you organize the information and simplifies the process of interpretation. While the full text of the law should be available for consideration and review, a simplified index enables you to focus on those essential issues affecting records retention.

- *Future updating.* The index usually contains the citations for each law. You can check the citations periodically for changes in the law. The process is much easier than analyzing the full text of the laws each time you update the research.

- *Expediting review and approval.* Your legal counsel must review the research. The index enables legal counsel to review the various citations and legal periods quickly when determining the accuracy of the retention schedule. Whenever a question arises, the full text of the legal requirement is available for review.

ORGANIZING THE INDEX ENTRIES

The most difficult part of creating the index is establishing the subject or function classifications. Use simple categories, with only a few options. The objective of the index is to bring similar laws together under a single code, rather than organize the universe of law (like the Dewey decimal system).

Some organizations successfully organize the laws by function (e.g., tax, employment, legal) rather than by subject. The functional index simplifies the process of extracting the legal requirements, grouping them, and then applying them to the Records Retention Schedule.

Make fine distinctions within classifications only when experience and knowledge indicate that certain legal requirements uniquely apply to specific records within your organization. For example, a state public utilities commission might have a specific requirement for customer records. Since this might be the only legal requirement that covers customer records, you might provide a special subject classification for this topic.

A computer database management system works best. The sorting capability of the computer enables you to organize information by subject, citation, record type, or any other method. For example, during the annual review of the legal research, the index can be sorted by citation so that each can be carefully reviewed for its continued applicability. Or, sort the database by agency so that their specific requirements can be examined. If you do not use a computer database, you can record the index information initially on index cards.

THE LEGAL PERIODS

Appendix E provides details regarding the abbreviations for legal periods. Chapter 4 provides details regarding the types of legal periods found in laws. Chapter 6 provides details regarding the creation of legal retention periods from legal periods.

You prepare the legal periods for the Legal Research Index after reading and analyzing the laws. You then translate the laws into abbreviations that summarize the legal periods. Legal counsel can review these abbreviations much faster than reading the full text of the laws and performing the legal analysis again.

The legal periods reflect *the content of the laws*, not their meaning for retention purposes. Do not convert these legal periods to legal retention periods at this time. You will later analyze these legal periods in the Legal Group File and determine how long to keep records for legal purposes.

Chapter 6   The Legal Group File

See Chapter 4 for details about legal research. See Chapter 5 for details about the Legal Research Index.

After you complete the legal research and prepare the Legal Research Index you can create the Legal Group File. The Legal Group File contains "a summary of legal requirements and legal considerations, in a simplified form, for use in the Records Retention Schedule."

Figure 6-2 shows a typical Legal Group File. Note that the example divides the legal periods into the legal requirements and legal considerations.

HOW TO PREPARE THE LEGAL GROUP FILE.

☐ Sort the Legal Research Index by subject.

☐ Create legal groups that summarize the major subjects in the Legal Research Index.

Use index cards for manual indexes.

☐ Prepare the Legal Group File entries.

☐ Sort the Legal Group File by legal group code.

☐ Print the Legal Group File.

☐ Assign the appropriate legal group codes to the Legal Research Index.

☐ Sort the Legal Research Index by legal group code, jurisdiction and citation.

☐ Print the Legal Research Index.

Figure 6-1. Contents and Abbreviations for the Legal Group File

CONTENTS

Create the Legal Group File from the information contained in the Legal Research Index. The Legal Group File contains the following information:

Legal Group Code. The unique code assigned to each legal group. Generally use an alpha-numeric code to identify the subject matter of the laws and the hierarchy.

Subject. The brief two- or three-line hierarchical subject identification of the content of the laws in the legal group.

Description. The scope of laws covered in the legal group.

Legal Requirements. The legal periods that express retention requirements— i.e., provisions that must be followed.

Legal Considerations. The legal periods that express considerations— i.e., provisions that affect your records but do not state requirements.

Total. The total retention period for legal purposes.

The Legal Group File may also contain detailed information taken from the Legal Research Index to facilitate review and analysis such as the minimum, maximum, and selected citations and the legal periods for both legal requirements and legal considerations.

ABBREVIATIONS (See Appendix E for details.)

Legal Periods: Minimum / Maximum

ATX:	ACT+TAX, active plus tax filing date.
AS:	limitation of assessment.
CY:	current year.
D:	days.
LA:	limitation of action.
IND:	indefinite.
MAINT:	maintain.
M:	months.
SL:	statute of limitations.
TAX:	tax filing date.
Y:	years.
number:	period of time
+:	plus.

Legal Retention Periods: Selected / Total

ACT:	active.
ACY:	ACT+CY, active plus current year.
CY:	current year.
D:	days.
IND:	indefinite.
M:	months.
Y:	years.
number:	period of time
+:	plus.

Express time periods in years, unless the law specifies months or days.

Figure 6-2. Sample Legal Group File

Legal Group	Subject	Description	Legal Requirements	Legal Considerations	Total
ACC000	Accounting / Tax General	Includes tax assessment or specific tax requirements for accounts payable, accounts receivable, etc.			
		Legal Requirements: **Minimum** TX: TTC 111.0041	3		
		Maximum US: 26 CFR 31.6001-1	4		
		Selected US: 26 CFR 31.6001-1	4		
		Legal Considerations: **Minimum** US: 26 USC 6532			
		Maximum US: 26 CFR 301.6501(C)-1		LA1	
		Selected US: 26 CFR 301.6501(E)-1		ASIND	
		Selected Legal Retention Period		6	6
ACC100	Accounting / Tax Capital Acquisitions	Includes depreciation, capital gains and losses, and repairs for capital property			
		Legal Requirements: **Minimum** US: 26 CFR 1.167(E)-1	ACT		
		Maximum US: 26 CFR 1.167(E)-1	ACT		
		Selected US: 26 CFR 1.167(E)-1	ACT		
		Legal Considerations: **Minimum** US: 26 CFR 301.6501(A)-1			
		Maximum US: 26 CFR 301.6501(C)-1		AS3	
		Selected US: 26 CFR 301.6501(A)-1		IND	
		Selected Legal Retention Period		6	ACT+6
ADV000	Advertising Packaging / Labeling	Includes laws related to promotions, introductory offers, product size advantages, etc. See MAN100 for product liability considerations.			
		Legal Requirements: **Minimum** US: 16 CFR 502.101	1		
		Maximum US: 16 CFR 502.101	1		
		Selected US: 16 CFR 502.101	1		
		Legal Considerations: **Minimum** TX: 16.003			
		Maximum TX: 16.003		LA2	
		Selected TX: 16.003 / LIABILITY CONCERNS		LA2	
		Selected Legal Retention Period		ACT+2	ACT+2

CREATING THE LEGAL GROUPS

You first sort the Legal Research Index by function or subject. This brings together the laws applicable to the same types of issues, regardless of jurisdiction or source. You then assign *the same legal group code* to all those laws that will be treated the same for records retention purposes.

Some government agencies issue unique or detailed requirements for a particular industry. In those cases, assign special legal group codes to represent those unique laws that cannot be grouped with others for records retention purposes. Expect some modifications in the legal group codes as you develop the records retention program.

The Legal Group File contains information about each legal group including the legal group code, subject, description, minimum and maximum legal periods, and selected and total legal retention periods. It distinguishes between legal requirements and legal considerations, and states the total legal retention period to be applied in the Records Retention Schedule.

LEGAL PERIODS AFFECTING RETENTION

See Appendix E for details regarding abbreviations for legal periods.

Each legal period shown in Figure 6-2 actually consists of two periods—the legal requirements period and the legal considerations period. The legal requirements period represents the time an organization must keep records to avoid fines, penalties, or other adverse consequences.

The legal considerations period represents one or more legal issues that might affect the retention of records. *These are not requirements!* Typically, statutes of limitation, some limitations of assessment, and concerns related to litigation fall into this category. You may keep records during this period or you may destroy them. Your organization will decide based upon its needs and its risk analysis.

Legal Requirements

The legal requirements section of the Legal Group File represents the retention period that an organization usually must follow. Legal requirements must clearly specify the period for retaining records. Typically, the law will state "records covered by this section must be kept for 'X' years."

You are under no obligation, however, to retain records under a law, unless the law clearly states the retention period. Similarly, a government agency may not enforce a vague retention requirement. You must have clear notice before fines or penalties can be imposed upon you.

The minimum limitation of assessment for tax purposes should also be treated as a legal requirement. Most tax laws require you to keep records for the period the taxing agency may need them for the administration of the tax law. Under normal circumstances, the tax agency may need your records to assess your taxes only during the stated minimum period. For example, the Internal Revenue Service must assess your taxes within three years after you file a tax return. This minimum limitation of assessment period of three years should be considered as a legal requirement. You will be expected to maintain your tax records for at least that long.

Other limitation of assessment periods generally refer to special circumstances such as fraud or the inadvertent understatement of income by 25% or more. These are legal considerations. You will maintain or destroy these records based upon your assessment of risk.

See Chapter 3 for help in determining the scope of the legal research.

You do not follow the legal requirements for those states in which you do not do business nor for those agencies that do not regulate your activities. Some records managers mistakenly apply legal requirements issued by a regulatory agency that lacks authority over their organization. These laws do not apply to you and should not even appear in your Legal Research Index.

Use the Legal Research Index to determine the longest legal requirement that applies to your organization. Scan the index for entries that have the same legal group code. Most numeric legal periods are legal requirements.

Legal requirements will generally fall into one of the following categories:

See Appendix E for details about abbreviations for legal periods.

Treat the minimum limitation of assessment periods as legal requirements.

Legal periods reflect the wording in the laws. Legal retention periods reflect practical periods for keeping records to comply with the law. See Appendix E for additional information.

- Laws specifying specific numerical retention periods after the creation of the records. (Example: 3, 5)

- Laws specifying specific numerical retention periods after specific events. (Examples: CY+5, ACT, ACT+30, ATX+3, TAX+3)

- Limitation of assessment periods specifying the minimum period the tax agency can assess your taxes. (Example: AS3)

- Laws specifying long-term or permanent retention periods. (Example: IND)

List the longest and shortest of these legal requirements periods in your Legal Group File. Include the legal citation and the abbreviation for the legal periods. This will enable legal counsel and other reviewers to see the scope of your legal requirement and determine that the total legal retention period is adequate.

The selected legal requirements period should be converted into records retention period abbreviations that can be used in the Records Retention Schedule. For example, the longest legal requirement for tax purposes might specify that records must be kept for five (5) years after filing a tax return (TAX+5). You may then propose a retention period of six (6) years after the end of the calendar year (CY+6). This six-year period would provide one year for the year the return is filed plus the five-year retention required by the law. By convention, all records should be maintained during the year in which they were created. Translating the legal period into a legal retention period facilitates the implementation and practical operation of the retention program.

You may select legal requirements periods that are less than the longest period stated by law in the following circumstances:

- *The law specifies a retention period that is only a few months longer than the selected one.* In the above example, the law requires you to keep records for five years after you file the tax return. This approach normally results in a safe legal requirement period of six

(6) years—one year for the year of filing and five years required by the law. You choose instead to specify a retention period of five (5) years, recognizing that this period is three and one half months shorter than the legal requirements. Since most people file tax returns around April 15—three and one half months after the end of the tax year—you determine that you face a small risk of fines or penalties. Regardless, you determine that the tax agency has always audited your organization within five years and has never requested information after six years.

- *You only have minimum contact with the state that has the longest legal retention requirement.* You choose to ignore the requirements of the state with the longest retention period and select the next longest retention period. History has shown that the second longest retention period has been adequate to protect your organization.

The Legal Group File may also indicate other reasons for selecting the legal requirements period. This will enable you to explain any deviations from the longest legal requirements period.

Legal Considerations

See Appendix F for additional information on how you apply risk assessment principles when determining the legal consideration periods.

Legal considerations include laws and other legal concerns that may impact the legal retention period. Use your discretion to determine whether records should be maintained during a legal consideration period or destroyed. If you destroy records in the regular course of business, under an approved records retention program, prior to litigation, government investigation or audit, you will not be subject to fines and penalties. On the other hand, if you destroy records too early, these records may not be available to help your organization defend itself during litigation and tax audits. Organizations have also found that keeping records too long may also be harmful in similar situations.

Legal considerations will generally fall into the following categories:

- *Statute of limitations or limitation of actions periods specifying when a legal action or lawsuit may be initiated.* (Example: SL3)

- *Limitation of assessment periods for taxes that specifies an unlikely occurrence.* For example, the Internal Revenue Service may assess your taxes up to six years after you file your tax return if you understate your income by 25% or more. It is unlikely that you will ever understate your income by that amount. Your risks are extremely small if you maintain tax records less than six years. (Example: LA6)

- *Laws containing requirements to keep records without stating specific records retention periods.* The retention periods for these records are generally presumed to be three years or less. (Example: MAINT)

- *Other concerns related to ongoing legal liability such as exposure of employees to hazardous substances or product liability.* Your organization may be held liable for damages for an indefinite period into the future. You should adopt a legal strategy to determine how long to keep records when it is unclear if or when you will be held liable. Sometimes concerns related to litigation will result in very long legal consideration periods. (Example: LA–IND for product liability since the statute of limitations could apply for an indefinite period into the future.)

See Appendix E for details
regarding abbreviations
for legal and records
retention periods.

The Legal Research Index contains abbreviations of the periods stated in the laws. Normally by scanning the laws under each legal group, you can determine the minimum and maximum legal consideration period.

The total legal consideration period will generally be one of the following:

- The longest legal considerations period,

- The shortest legal considerations period,

- The average or mean legal considerations period,

- The legal considerations period that is longer than 80% of the other legal consideration periods, or

- The period you or your legal counsel feels is appropriate.

Again, these periods are not legal requirements and you do not have to keep records during these periods. You are therefore free to select any legal consideration period that protects your organization. Include citations for the minimum, maximum and selected periods. You may need to convert the selected legal considerations period into a records retention period that you can use in the Records Retention Schedule.

Identify the legal considerations period independent of the legal requirements period. This will enable you and your legal counsel to differentiate between the retention periods for legal considerations and legal requirements purposes.

The Legal Group File may also indicate other reasons for selecting the legal considerations period. This will enable you to explain any deviations from the longest legal considerations period.

Total Legal Retention Periods

You will later transfer the total legal retention period to the appropriate retention categories in the Records Retention Schedule. See Chapter 7 for details.

You can now compare the selected retention periods for legal requirements and legal considerations. The longest of those two retention periods will become the total legal retention period for the legal group.

Legal Periods Versus Legal Retention Periods

See Appendix E for detail about legal periods and records retention periods.

You use legal periods from the Legal Research Index for the minimum and maximum periods for both legal requirements and legal considerations. These periods reflect the actual periods stated in the laws.

You convert legal periods to legal retention periods for the selected legal requirements and legal considerations periods and the total legal retention period. Legal retention periods reflect your interpretation of the legal requirements and considerations. They represent your analysis and understanding of what the laws mean and how long your records should be kept. The legal retention periods also provide specific retention instructions—keep the records for 3 years—rather than the detailed, confusing language of the laws.

Why Analyze the Legal Periods

While the procedures described above may seem cumbersome, they will result in an accurate determination of your legal retention periods. Many organizations do not understand the difference between legal requirements and legal considerations. As a result, some organizations keep records for long periods of time because someone mistakenly believes that a legal consideration, such as a statute of limitation, states a retention requirement.

The methodology described above clearly differentiates between legal requirements and legal considerations. You must normally apply the longest legal requirement without discretion. You may use your discretion only when applying legal considerations. Emphasize this difference during the review period.

This process also enables you to modify legal retention periods quickly and easily if circumstances change. For example, if an organization ceases to do business in a state with the longest legal requirement, you can quickly determine the second longest legal requirement from the Legal Research Index and change the total retention for the associated legal groups. You then apply the new legal retention periods to your Records Retention Schedule. Similarly, if attitudes change toward legal considerations, you can change the legal retention periods to correspond to the new position.

THE LEGAL GROUP FILE WITHOUT DETAILED ANALYSIS

Figure 6-3 provides an example of the Legal Group File without the detailed information regarding minimum, maximum and selected legal requirements and legal considerations. This report is often useful to provide reviewers with information about the legal group process. By eliminating the detail, you may avoid confusing the reviewers regarding the legal research or legal analysis you performed. Legal counsel should still review the version of the Legal Group File that contains the detailed analysis.

Figure 6-3. Sample Legal Group File Without Detailed Analysis

Legal Group	Subject	Description	Legal Requirements	Legal Considerations	Total
ACC000	Accounting / Tax General	Includes tax assessment or specific tax requirements for accounts payable, accounts receivable, etc.	4	6	6
ACC100	Accounting / Tax Capital Acquisitions	Includes depreciation, capital gains and losses, and repairs for capital property	ACT	6	ACT+6
ADV000	Advertising Packaging / Labeling	Includes laws related to promotions, introductory offers, product size advantages, etc. See MAN100 for product liability considerations.	1	ACT+2	ACT+2
BUS000	Business Organization General	Includes requirements for articles of incorporation, partnership documentation, etc. Excludes meeting minutes, shareholder information, etc.	3	IND	IND
BUS010	Business Organization Former Organizations	Includes requirements for articles of incorporation, partnership documentation, etc. Excludes meeting minutes, shareholder information, etc.	3	10	10
BUS100	Business Organization Corporation Organization Documentation	Includes requirements for articles of incorporation, partnership documentation, etc. Excludes meeting minutes, shareholder information, etc.	3	IND	IND
BUS110	Business Organization Corporation Shareholder Records	Includes stock transactions, shareholder addresses, etc. Retention established based upon liability to shareholders for failure to send notices, dividends, etc., and rights granted by ownership agreements, including purchase of stock.	3	ACT+10	ACT+10
BUS120	Business Organization Corporation Meetings	Includes minutes and notices from board, shareholder, and committee meetings.	3	10	10

Chapter 7   The Records Retention Schedule

The Records Retention Schedule is the central feature of the entire records retention program. It specifies how long your organization will keep records and who will maintain them. You use the Records Retention Schedule to determine when to destroy records.

See Appendix A for additional pages from this Records Retention Schedule.

Figure 7-2 shows a sample page from the Records Retention Schedule.

HOW TO PREPARE THE RECORDS RETENTION SCHEDULE

☐ Sort the records inventory into groups of related records.

Use index cards for manual programs.

☐ Develop initial retention categories, codes and descriptions based upon your knowledge of your organization and your records.

☐ Revise the retention categories until each entry from the records inventory can be assigned to the appropriate retention category.

☐ Sort the retention categories in order of the retention codes.

Transfer the legal retention period from the Legal Group File for the legal group code assigned.

☐ Assign the appropriate legal group codes from the Legal Group File.

Figure 7-1. Contents and Abbreviations for the Records Retention Schedule

CONTENTS

Create the Records Retention Schedule from information obtained from the records inventory, interviews with record users, the Legal Group File and your knowledge of the organization.

Retention Category Code. The unique alpha-numeric code to identify the subject matter and the hierarchy.

Retention Category. The two- or three-line hierarchical subject or functional definition of the records series covered.

Legal Group Code. The legal group code from the Legal Group File that identifies the group of laws affecting this category.

Description. The scope of records covered or excluded.

Cross Reference. Other retention categories to be checked for related records or for records excluded from each category.

Retention of Official Records. The retention period that applies to official records maintained by the segment of the organization specified in the "Office of Record" column.

Legal Retention Period. The retention period for legal purposes. This period is taken from the Legal Group File.

User Retention Period. The retention period for user purposes.

Other Retention Period. The retention period for historical, research or other purposes.

Total Retention Period. The total retention period.

Retention of Copies. The retention period for records maintained by everyone not specified in the "Office of Record" column.

Office of Record. The segment or segments of the organization responsible for keeping the official set of records.

ABBREVIATIONS (See Appendix E for details.)

ACT:	active.	SUP:	superseded
ACY:	ACT+CY, active plus current year.	Y:	years.
CY:	current year.	*number*:	period of time
D:	days.	+:	plus.
IND:	indefinite.		
MAX:	maximum.		
M:	months.		

Express time periods in years, unless the law specifies months or days.

Figure 7-2. Sample Records Retention Schedule

Retention Code	Retention Category Description / Cross Reference	Legal Group	Retention of Official Records				Retention of Copies	Office of Record
			Legal	User	Other	Total		
ACC1000	**Accounting** **Accounts Payable/Receivable** Records related to payment of financial obligations and receipt of revenues. Includes vouchers, vendor invoices and statements; payroll and payroll deductions; government contracts and grants, contributions, and other income.	ACC000	6	3	0	6	MAX1	Accounting
ACC1010	**Accounting** **Journals / Ledgers** Records used to transfer charges between accounts and for summarizing account information. Final, annual records only.	ACC000	6	10	0	10	MAX1	Accounting
ACC2000	**Accounting** **Capital Property** Includes purchase and sales of property and equipment, depreciation, improvements, etc. Includes financial obligations associated with capital expenditures, purchase of land, buildings, equipment, furnishings, motor vehicles; material transfers, work orders, additions or improvements to building or equipment, property reporting.	ACC100	ACT+6	ACT	0	ACT+6	MAX5	Accounting
ACC9900	**Accounting** **General** Records related to accounting records not previously covered. Includes accounting reports, control documents; system input, maintenance and changes.	NONE	0	3	0	3	MAX1	Accounting

☐ Assign the appropriate user retention periods, total retention periods, copy retention periods, and office of record.

☐ Review and revise the information for each retention category.

☐ Print the Records Retention Schedule.

THE FUNCTIONAL RETENTION SCHEDULE

The manner in which you organize and present the Records Retention Schedule to record users may also determine whether the program will ultimately comply with the law. The program will not operate properly if the Records Retention Schedule is poorly organized, inaccurate, cannot readily be used to find appropriate information, and cannot be revised and updated quickly and accurately. Records that could and should be destroyed in the ordinary course of business may not be destroyed or may be destroyed improperly. Errors may result that compromise the records destruction process. The entire records retention program may not withstand close legal scrutiny.

The functional retention schedule, sometimes referred to as the "general retention schedule," simplifies the process of creating and maintaining a Records Retention Schedule, and improves your accuracy in the process. While traditional Records Retention Schedules claim to be organized by "record series," many are actually organized by record titles. You organize the functional Records Retention Schedule by the functions performed by your organization. In some cases, a functional category may represent a single record series; in other cases, the functional category may consolidate several record series. This type of retention schedule contains fewer, but broader, retention categories.

A functional retention category can be better understood through an example using accounting records. An accounting department produces several different records including ledgers, journals, invoices, statements, vouchers, canceled checks, bank statements, bills, and payroll. Realistically, these records all serve one major function: to properly account for income and expenses.

From a legal perspective, these same records serve to support information presented in the tax returns submitted to the Internal Revenue Service or state revenue departments. In the government sector, this information serves to support government audits. Although accounting encompasses many different record titles used by different people within the entire organization, the records still support the same functional purpose.

In most traditional, detailed Records Retention Schedules, each different type of record related to the accounting function would be listed separately, probably under the accounting department. If another department creates or maintains similar accounting records, the records would also appear under that department heading. A separate retention period would be assigned to each record type and a separate legal justification provided.

In some detailed, traditional retention schedules, different retention periods would be assigned based upon perceived differences in value for the records. For example, detailed bills, statements, and vouchers related to accounts payable may be kept for up to six years after the tax return is filed while the resulting general ledger may be kept "permanently" because of perceived difference in value. Even the detailed records related to the actual amounts due may be kept for different periods of time. It is not surprising that this type of records retention schedule is confusing, time consuming, and often inaccurate.

In contrast, the functional retention approach treats all records related to the accounting function in the same way. No breakdown by department is even necessary. No distinctions are made between one type of record versus another within the accounting function, unless there is a compelling reason for a different period.

In our accounting example, capital acquisitions and property records will be treated as a separate functional category. Since the taxable gain or loss for property is dependent upon the purchase price, depreciation, and value of improvements made to the property prior to its sale or disposition, you should normally keep these types of records from the "time of their creation" or "while they are active," until you sell or dispose of the property. You then keep them for the retention period followed for other accounting records.

The only two functional categories actually required for accounting records are as follows:

Retention Code	Retention Category	Description	Retention Period
ACC000	Accounting General	Includes all general accounting records maintained for tax purposes, including accounts payable, accounts receivable, payroll, banking, etc.	6
ACC100	Accounting Capital Property	Includes purchase documents, depreciation, capital gains and losses related to capital property.	ACT+6

Figure 7-2 provides an example page from this type of Records Retention Schedule. Some organizations prefer to divide the general accounting function into areas such as accounts receivable, accounts payable, and payroll, although they will all have the same retention period.

ADVANTAGES

The functional retention schedule has the following features that make it particularly attractive:

- *The functional retention schedule is relatively easy to develop.* The functional retention schedule can be developed quickly. Many functional areas can be determined by examining an organization chart, interviewing people within each functional group, and through experience from a knowledge of an organization.

- *The functional retention schedule can be developed with a minimal inventory.* Most traditional, detailed records retention schedules require an extensive records inventory. This ensures that the records retention schedule lists all the records with the corresponding retention periods.

Some organizations manage the records retention program with only the functional retention schedule. Chapter 8 indicates how you can also assign retention periods to the records listed in the inventory.

A functional retention schedule uses the inventory only to help you establish the appropriate retention categories. As indicated above, many functional categories can be developed without even using an inventory. A simplified listing of records may be adequate to demonstrate that retention categories are broad enough to cover the various types of records. You can assign a retention category code to each record in the inventory to confirm the accuracy of the functional retention schedule and provide a cross reference between the record titles and their related retention categories.

- *The functional Records Retention Schedule normally contains under 100 retention categories.* The typical functional retention schedule for even a large organization will contain under 100 different retention categories—many will contain between 50 and 70 categories. Many of these categories can be developed at the beginning of the project. A few will be added or revised to accommodate special circumstances.

- *The functional retention schedule is more consistent since you group a large number of record titles into one retention category.* In a traditional, detailed Records Retention Schedule, all record titles are listed and a retention period assigned to each. Since similar records may appear anywhere within the retention schedule, they can inadvertently be assigned inconsistent retention periods.

- *The functional retention schedule generally provides only one category for related records.* Most record titles will fall within one retention category. For example, the functional category "Contracts" provides a single retention period for all contracts including employment contracts, consulting contracts, service contracts, equipment contracts and all other types of contracts.

Chapter 2 describes the 80/20 rule. Since the functional retention schedule can be produced faster than traditional methods, you can spend the remaining 80 percent of your time fine-tuning the program and resolving conflicts.

In a few cases, records may fall within two or more categories—but generally less than 10% to 20% of the time. As the functional retention schedule evolves, these problems can be reduced or eliminated. In most traditional retention schedules, confusion regarding which retention period to apply usually occurs more often.

- *The functional retention schedule operates independently of the organizational structure.* It does not have to be revised when your organization changes.

  The functional retention schedule organizes information by functional activity, rather than organizational structure. Sometimes the functional activity will be unique to a particular department. For example, the "Construction" function is unique within the engineering department. In other cases, the functional activity will cross departmental lines. For example, while the accounting department and personnel department are primarily responsible for accounting and personnel matters respectively, every other segment of the organization also performs these functions.

- *The functional retention schedule specifies the segment of the organization that maintains the official set of records.* The "office of record" is the department or group with the responsibility for maintaining the "official" version of the record for the total retention period. All other groups that perform the same function, maintain unofficial or nonrecord copies. Based upon the needs of record users, these copies can be destroyed after a shorter period. Some organizations send records to the office of record location prior to destruction to ensure that the office of record location has a full set of appropriate records.

- *The functional retention schedule is easier to maintain.* Since you base the functional retention schedule on the evaluation of many laws and many records, you will rarely need to change the retention periods in the future. When appropriate, a few exceptions may be added to the functional categories to provide for special circumstances. You can devote time instead for special problems rather than continuing maintenance of the retention schedule.

LEGAL RETENTION PERIODS

Assign the legal group code "NONE" or "NLR" (no legal requirement) to those retention categories not affected by any laws.

The *Skupsky Retention Method* simplifies that assignment of legal retention periods to the Records Retention Schedule. You first determine the types of laws that affect each retention category and assign the appropriate legal group code from the Legal Group File. The retention period assigned to the legal group will then apply to the retention category. One legal retention period from the Legal Group File may apply to several retention categories, affecting perhaps hundreds of record titles.

The advantage of this process is as follows:

- You assign only one legal group code to represent many laws affecting the retention category.

- You only assign one legal group code to the retention category, instead of assigning individual laws to individual records in that category.

In a manual system, you change the legal and total retention periods for the retention categories affected when you change the legal retention period for the legal group. In computer systems, the retention periods for the Records Retention Schedule can automatically change when the legal retention period in the Legal Group File changes.

- If the legal retention period changes, the legal and total retention periods for the retention category also change. This procedure is a lot easier than having to change each retention period in the traditional, detailed retention schedule.

- You assign fewer legal retention periods with this procedure, resulting in fewer decisions and greater accuracy.

- By assigning a summarized legal group requirement to a functional category, you reduce the chances of error related to the legal retention period.

USER RETENTION PERIODS

You also assign user retention periods to the retention categories. Since the user retention periods for the retention categories reflect the needs of many record users, records within the category will probably be kept "long enough." Granted, some records may be kept "too long"—although only by a few years.

You can develop exceptions to the functional records categories to eliminate these kinds of problems.

Organizations create and maintain records so that employees have the records they need to do their jobs and help meet the goals of the organization. Additionally, organizations create records to comply with applicable laws.

Unfortunately, many people confuse these two issues: records created to meet the needs of the organization versus records created to comply with the law. In reality, both issues must be considered independently when developing a records retention program. For each entry in the Records Retention Schedule, one period should be established to identify user or operational requirements—the period for keeping records solely to meet the needs of the organization. Another period should be established for legal issues—the legal requirements or considerations for retaining records. The total retention period is the longest of these two periods. Figure 7-2 shows these three retention periods in a sample Records Retention Schedule.

User Needs Versus Legal Concerns

The user retention period reflects the period the organization needs the records so that employees can do their jobs. You create accounts receivable records, for example, initially to help account for, bill and collect money owed by outside groups. These records have little or no value after payment, except to respond to inquiries. Similarly, accounts payable records have little value after the other party cashes the checks and properly credits the payments. In both cases, the user retention periods would be only one to two years.

Record users often confuse this type of retention assessment with legal issues that also might affect the records. The following legal issues should not be confused with user issues:

- The period your organization needs records for tax purposes.

- The potential need for the records during future litigation.

- The requirements of state or federal regulatory agencies.

You should remind record users that their user retention periods do not include any legal concerns. The legal department will actively review the Records Retention Schedule to ensure that the appropriate legal periods have been assigned to each retention category. The users are the experts to determine how long they need records to do their job; the lawyers are the experts to determine how long the records should be kept to meet legal obligations.

User Retention Criteria

The user retention periods are subjective in nature. Objective criteria rarely apply to help you determine how long users need the records to do their jobs. When developing traditional records retention programs, the record users are often first asked to recommend retention periods. Unfortunately, record users often respond with retention periods that are too long. Once these longer periods have been expressed or, even worse, printed on a draft of the Records Retention Schedule, it is difficult to undo the damage.

Record users have a right to retain records for the period they need the records to do their jobs. The organization, on the other hand, has the same interest to keep records long enough to meet the needs of the organization but it also has a right to ensure that they are not kept any longer. The decision to keep records for long periods increases costs, requires more staff, reduces access to valuable records and may create problems in litigation. You should therefore base user retention periods upon "actual" rather than "perceived" needs.

Interviewing Record Users

Many records management books and articles describe the traditional approach for developing Records Retention Schedules and in particular for determining the user retention periods. Most of these sources suggest that the best way to determine user retention periods is by asking the actual users. Since they are the ones who use the records, these sources surmise, they are the ones most likely to know how long these records should be kept.

While this approach seems good in theory, it is sometimes ineffective for the following reasons:

- Before the interview, users rarely think about how long they need the records.

- When asked how long to keep the records, users will tend to respond with a conservative answer such as "forever" or for other long periods of time. They believe this is a "safe" answer because the records will be available whenever needed in the future.

- In spite of everything the interviewer may tell them, users still tend to confuse legal retention with user retention as described above.

- Users normally will not dedicate the time to review each record series or group of records nor suggest user retention periods.

- Users have an unrealistic view of the importance of their records. Either they created the records themselves or believe the organization would suffer if they destroy even one piece of paper.

For these reasons, *do not ask the record users to even suggest retention periods during the interview!* Instead, take this opportunity to assess their general attitudes toward records retention. You can ask them for a brief description of the records they use. Most record users confirm that they actually need their records for only a short time. After this initial period, they rarely need the records again.

Another important question to ask during an interview is "how far back the user has ever gone to retrieve records and for what purpose?" You will often find that they access records older than five or ten years merely to respond to inquiries. What would have happened if those records did not exist? Realistically, the person requesting information would have no choice but to proceed without the information. Rarely would the organization suffer severe circumstances.

In summary, the following types of questions would be appropriate for an initial interview with the record users:

- What types of records does your department maintain?

- How do you use these records?

- Describe some circumstances when you needed records after three years? After five years? After ten years?

- What would have happened if you could not find the records or they no longer existed?

With the interviewee's permission, you might record the interview on tape instead of taking notes. This will allow for the free flow of information without interruptions. You will also be able to devote your full attention to listening to the responses and preparing other questions.

After the interview, assess the general needs and temperament of the various record users. This will be useful in establishing the preliminary user retention periods.

Assigning the Preliminary User Retention Periods

Determine the preliminary user retention periods based upon your interview with the record users, your knowledge of the organization, and your experience with specific records. These preliminary periods should represent your practical assessment of the needs of record users. These periods will often be much shorter than the user would normally state if asked.

You may also examine your previous Records Retention Schedules to get some idea of how long records should be kept for user purposes. Unfortunately, many old retention schedules do not distinguish between user and legal retention periods, and therefore may not be appropriate for this purpose.

Revising the User Retention Periods

After you finish the preliminary version of the Records Retention Schedule, distribute copies for comments. The copies should be printed in final format. Use your desktop publishing or laser printing capabilities if available. Do not even mark the copies as "draft." Make the readers feel that they are reviewing the final version. They may then feel compelled only to suggest changes based upon sound reasons.

You are asking the record users to "react" to the user retention periods stated, rather than suggesting their own initial periods. You might ask the following question in the form stated:

> Explain why a user retention period, if any, in the Records Retention Schedule does not meet your needs. Do not consider any of the legal retention periods. The legal department is handling all legal issues.

The form of the question is important. You want to determine only why a user retention period does not meet the user's needs, not how long does the user want to keep these records. You also want to reassure the users that the user periods are probably correct. There may be no problems at all with the user retention periods.

Most users will be hard pressed to articulate reasons for keeping records for long periods when the preliminary user retention period indicates only "three years." Psychologically, they need to identify valid reasons for longer retention periods or they will appear silly or arbitrary. People also tend not to change written documents — especially if they look typeset. This type of subtle pressure forces record users to take a more realistic look at their records retention needs. It helps ensure that records will be kept only for the period needed, but no longer.

This approach also enables the users to see the actual difference between the columns for the user and legal retention periods. The users can then determine their user retention periods confident that the legal department will determine the retention periods in the legal column.

One disadvantage of this approach is that users might tend to increase the user retention periods "to be safe," if the legal periods are longer. You can help the users resist this temptation by reinforcing the basis for the user retention periods— the period the users need the records to do their jobs — not the periods required by law.

Negotiating the User Retention Periods

Since the user retention periods are subjective, you will negotiate the final periods. If you follow the procedures stated above, the chances are good that the user retention periods will be reasonable in terms of the users' actual need. Sometimes the user still wants longer retention periods "just in case" or because the proposed periods are just not adequate.

Let the users articulate any legitimate reasons for changing the user retention periods. After a detailed discussion of the user's concern, you may either accept the new periods suggested by the users or offer compromises.

Users want to feel that you considered their views. They may even feel that "they really got away with one" when you compromise on a retention period perhaps two or three years higher than the initial period that you previously suggested. Through discussion and compromise the revised user retention periods will tend to be significantly lower than the periods users would normally suggest if asked initially.

You should negotiate user periods that are perhaps a little less than the users propose but long enough to meet the users' perceived needs. If nothing else, you should strive to establish a specific numerical period such as "50 years" rather than "permanent." You can then destroy records at a specific time in the future, even if that time is long after the record's actual useful life has ended.

In addition, by stating a specific retention period, you can periodically review this retention period in relationship to the users' actual needs for records. Many records management software programs will track access to the organization's records. By maintaining logs over time, you can document the actual records usage. Every few years, meet with the record users to compare their actual usage with their perceived user retention periods. Even if you initially accepted a compromise retention period of 50 years to gain acceptance for the overall records retention program, you can still review that decision every few years. You can then negotiate lower retention periods based upon the actual usage for records. Over time, the user retention periods will then approach the actual needs of the organization.

Your Responsibility to Record Users

Since you only ask record users to react to user retention periods, they may only request changes to periods that are obviously erroneous. If record users do not review the proposed schedules carefully, some records may be destroyed prematurely and the organization may suffer severe consequences.

Some may view this approach to user retention periods as pompous or presumptuous. This approach assumes that you, the records manager or retention system designer, are better able initially to determine the user retention periods than the record users. Actually, that is often true since most record users do not have expertise in records retention. Some may not have a realistic attitude toward the value of their records and others may not have the time to devote to this task. But you can also harm your organization if you only try to gain acceptance for the lowest possible user retention periods, instead of the most appropriate ones.

You are therefore responsible also to safeguard the process. First, understand the needs and operation of your organization before developing user retention periods. This will take time, study and dedication. Then, make sure that the appropriate record users review the retention schedule in depth. Keep after them until you are certain that the user retention periods are realistic and will meet the needs of your organization. Only then can you feel confident in the validity of the user retention periods.

OTHER RETENTION PERIODS

Some organizations also establish retention periods for research, historical or other purposes. The private sector considers research as part of the user retention periods, and rarely even considers historical issues because of the cost and time involved. In contrast, the government sector considers both these issues important in determining the total retention for records.

TOTAL RETENTION PERIODS

See Appendix E for additional information about records retention periods and abbreviations, including rules and exception on how to determine the total retention period.

The total retention period is the longest of the legal, user and other retention periods. For records retention calculation purposes, the alphabetic retention periods below appear in descending order of length:

- IND (indefinite)

- ACY (active plus current year)

- ACT (active)

- SUP (superseded)

- MAX (maximum)

- CY (current year)

You generally add the longest numerical period to the longest alphabetic period to get the total retention period:

Legal Period	User Period	TOTAL Period
3	4	4
ACT+3	6	ACT+6
ACT+3	ACT+4	ACT+4

OFFICE OF RECORD

Try to identify one group or entity in your organization who will be responsible for maintaining the official set of records for each retention category. This will often be the group that created the records or the one that needs the records for the longest period.

Records in certain retention categories — contracts, project files, and general administrative records — will be maintained by multiple segments of your organization. You can use a code such as "Various" or "All" to indicate that records in this category are maintained is multiple locations. One set in each location should be retained for the period stated for the total retention period for official records. Duplicate copies may be destroyed in each location according to the retention period for copies.

RETENTION PERIODS FOR COPIES

Segments of your organization, other than the one identified in the "Office of Record," maintain the records for the period stated for copies. This retention period for copies will never be longer than the retention period for official records.

IMPACT ON YOUR ACTIVE FILING SYSTEM

The retention categories also represent possible categories for organizing the active filing system. Sometimes the same categories can be used for both active filing and records retention purposes. In other cases, some additional subdivisions will be required.

Ideally, the active filing system should be compatible with the Records Retention Schedule. This enables the orderly movement of records from active filing, to remote storage, and to ultimate destruction. The functional approach to both filing and records retention brings this ideal closer to reality. Regardless, the information gained in developing the functional retention schedule will help dramatically in developing the active filing system.

Chapter 8

The Records Listing With Retention Periods

Chapter 7 for details about the Records Retention Schedule. Chapter 3 provides details on preparing the Records Inventory.

The Records Listing With Retention Periods specifies the records retention periods for record series identified in the records inventory. You first assign the retention and category code from the Records Retention Schedule to each record series. The records retention period from the Records Retention Schedule becomes the records retention period for the record series.

Appendix B provides an expanded example.

Figure 8-2 shows a sample page from the Records Listing With Retention Periods organized by department and record series.

HOW TO PREPARE THE RECORDS LISTING WITH RETENTION PERIODS

Follow these steps to prepare the Records Listing With Retention Periods:

☐ Sort the records inventory alphabetically by organization entity name and record series name.

☐ Assign the appropriate retention category code from the Records Retention Schedule to each record series.

For manual systems, transfer the corresponding retention periods from the Records Retention Schedule.

☐ Print the Records Listing using the retention periods for the appropriate retention category taken from the Records Retention Schedule.

CONTENTS

Create the Records Listing With Retention Periods by assigning entries in the records inventory to retention categories in the Records Retention Schedule.

Department/Location. The department, location or other segment of the organization that maintains the records.

Record Series. The name or title you assign to a group of similar or related records, used or filed as a unit. You identify the record series initially in the records inventory.

Record Code. The code your organization assigns to identify each record or record series. Some organization assign unique filing codes for records. Others may use the unique number assigned to each records inventory form.

Retention Category. The applicable retention category code from the Records Retention Schedule.

Legal Group. The legal group code assigned to the retention category.

Retention of Official Records. The legal, user, other and total records retention periods for "official records" taken from the Records Retention Schedule.

Retention of Copies. The retention period for copies taken from the Records Retention Schedule.

Office of Record. The segment of the organization responsible for maintaining the "official records" as stated in the Records Retention Schedule. If the office of record is the same as the department or group in which this record series appears, then the "Retention of Official Records" period applies. Otherwise, the "Retention of Copies" period applies.

Status. The status of the records series: "official" versus "duplicates" or "copies." You determine the status when preparing the records inventory.

ABBREVIATIONS (See Appendix E for details.)

ACT:	active.	SUP:	superseded
ACY:	ACT+CY, active plus current year	Y:	years
CY:	current year	*number:*	period of time
D:	days	+:	plus
IND:	indefinite		
MAX:	maximum		
M:	months		

Express time periods in years, unless the law specifies months or days.

Figure 8-2. Sample Records Listing With Retention Periods

Department / Location Record Series	Record Code	Retention Category	Legal Group	Retention of Official Records — Legal	User	Other	Total	Retention of Copies	Office of Record	Status
Accounting										
Accounts Payable										
accounts payable	ACC-00-01	ACC1000	ACC000	6	3	0	6	MAX1	Accounting	Official
accounts payable invoices	ACC-00-02	ACC1000	ACC000	6	3	0	6	MAX1	Accounting	Official
accounts payable ledgers	ACC-00-03	ACC1010	ACC000	6	10	0	10	MAX1	Accounting	Official
amortization records	ACC-00-04	ACC1000	ACC000	6	3	0	6	MAX1	Accounting	Official
bills	ACC-00-05	ACC1000	ACC000	6	3	0	6	MAX1	Accounting	Official
cash disbursements	ACC-00-06	ACC1000	ACC000	6	3	0	6	MAX1	Accounting	Official
commission statements	ACC-00-07	MIS1000	NONE	0	1	0	1	MAX1	Various	Official
cost accounting records	ACC-00-08	ACC1000	ACC000	6	3	0	6	MAX1	Accounting	Official
cost sheets	ACC-00-09	ACC1000	ACC000	6	3	0	6	MAX1	Accounting	Official
cost statements	ACC-00-10	ACC1000	ACC000	6	3	0	6	MAX1	Accounting	Official
credit card charge slips	ACC-00-11	ACC1000	ACC000	6	3	0	6	MAX1	Accounting	Official
credit card statements	ACC-00-12	ACC1000	ACC000	6	3	0	6	MAX1	Accounting	Official
debit advices	ACC-00-13	ACC1000	ACC000	6	3	0	6	MAX1	Accounting	Official
donations	ACC-00-14	ACC1000	ACC000	6	3	0	6	MAX1	Accounting	Official
expense reports	ACC-00-15	ACC1000	ACC000	6	3	0	6	MAX1	Accounting	Official
invoices	ACC-00-16	ACC1000	ACC000	6	3	0	6	MAX1	Accounting	Official
petty cash records	ACC-00-17	ACC1000	ACC000	6	3	0	6	MAX1	Accounting	Official
property taxes	ACC-00-18	ACC1000	ACC000	6	3	0	6	MAX1	Accounting	Official
purchase requisitions	ACC-00-19	FIN8000	NONE	0	3	0	3	MAX1	Finance	Official
royalty payments	ACC-00-20	ACC1000	ACC000	6	3	0	6	MAX1	Accounting	Official
travel expenses	ACC-00-21	ACC1000	ACC000	6	3	0	6	MAX1	Accounting	Official
unemployment insurance payments	ACC-00-22	ACC1000	ACC000	6	3	0	6	MAX1	Accounting	Official
vouchers	ACC-00-23	ACC1000	ACC000	6	3	0	6	MAX1	Accounting	Official
workers compensation insurance payments	ACC-00-24	ACC1000	ACC000	6	3	0	6	MAX1	Accounting	Official
Accounts Receivable										
accounts receivable	ACC-10-01	ACC1000	ACC000	6	3	0	6	MAX1	Accounting	Official
accounts receivable ledgers	ACC-10-02	ACC1010	ACC000	6	10	0	10	MAX1	Accounting	Official
cash books	ACC-10-03	ACC1010	ACC000	6	10	0	10	MAX1	Accounting	Official

CREATING THE RECORDS LISTING

Remember, you determine
the records retention
periods in the Records
Retention Schedule, not
the Records Listing.

The Records Listing provides record users with a complete listing of their records, organized by department, with the appropriate records retention periods indicated. You can update this listing whenever the Records Retention Schedule changes.

You can realize several advantages through this approach:

- You can develop under 100 retention categories and periods—often 50 to 70—regardless of the number of record series in your organization.

- You can consistently assign similar records the same retention period.

- You can modify and update the retention periods for individual record series quickly and accurately. You just modify the Records Retention Schedule and transfer those changes to the corresponding items in the Records Listing.

- You can assign more accurate record retention periods assigned to individual record series.

- You can develop the Records Retention Program faster and more accurately.

You may also encounter some disadvantages with this approach:

- The records retention periods must be transferred from the Records Retention Schedule.

  In a manual system, this information must be transcribed from one report to the other. Proofread carefully to prevent errors. In a computerized relational database, the retention periods can be transferred automatically. You search the Records Retention Schedule for that retention code, and retrieve the corresponding retention period. You then print each Records Listing entry with the corresponding retention period.

- A records retention category in the Records Retention Schedule must exist that corresponds to each record series.

  If you find that a particular record series does not fall into any existing retention category, then create a new category or modify an existing one to accommodate the record series. Sometimes you will add a new retention category as an "exception" to an existing category.

  You normally first attempt to expand or modify an existing retention category to accommodate a particular record series, rather than adding a new one. The Records Retention Schedule should be kept as small as possible. Add a new category only when no other alternative proves successful.

- The Records Listing must be changed each time the organizational structure changes.

- This disadvantage represents a major reason for assigning the retention periods to retention categories in the Records Retention Schedule rather than to individual records.

  The Records Retention Schedule exists independently of the structure of your organization. It does not change when the organization changes. Actually, you could operate the records retention program using only the Records Retention Schedule. The Records Listing serves as an added convenience to users — it helps them determine the exact retention period for each record series. You may choose to discontinue the Records Listing if you find it burdensome to maintain.

With careful planning and accurate work, you can overcome these disadvantages.

ASSIGNING RETENTION CATEGORY CODES

Your Records Listing will contain the correct records retention period for each record series only if you successfully assign the correct records retention code. The following suggestions will help you assign the correct retention category codes:

- Read each retention category description until you are familiar with the structure of the Records Retention Schedule.

- Assign the retention category code to those record series from the records inventory that clearly and exclusively fall within the definitions in the Records Retention Schedule.

- Assign the more specific retention category when you could assign two or more retention categories to the same record series.

  Occasionally, you will find two or more retention categories that are broad enough to include a specific record series. You should first attempt to determine which of the two represents the more specific requirement. For example, under the functional category "Administration," you may have developed subcategories such as "Internal Services" and "General." Records related to computer system development should be assigned to the more specific retention category related to "Internal Services." You use the "General" category only for those items that do not fall under the functional category. Similarly, you use the category "Miscellaneous" only when the record does not fall under any other more specific category in the Records Retention Schedule.

Under normal circumstances, 80 to 90 percent of your record series will fall into only one specific category. In 10 to 20 percent of the cases, the record series will fall into two or more categories or maybe not into any category. When resolving the conflicts posed by these latter problems, make the fewest possible modifications to the Records Retention Schedule. Create the minimum number of retention categories to accommodate the needs of your organization.

You may still need to modify the Records Retention Schedule in the following circumstances:

- Modify the Records Retention Schedule when a record series can reasonably be assigned to two or more retention categories.

  If none of the possible retention categories proves specific enough, you must modify the Records Retention Schedule. First, try modifying the definitions to resolve the conflicts. Second, try specifying exceptions to all but one retention category with cross references to the category to which the record series should be assigned. Finally, if all else fails, create a new specific category to accommodate this exception.

- Modify the Records Retention Schedule when a record series cannot be assigned to any retention category.

  If you cannot determine any applicable retention category, first try to expand the definition of an existing category so that it includes the record series under consideration. If that proves impossible, you may then need to develop a new retention category, perhaps as an exception to an existing category.

SPECIAL REPORTS

Records Retention Schedule with Records Listing

Figure 8-3 shows the Records Retention Schedule with a listing of records assigned to each retention category. You will find this type of report valuable to review whether you assigned each record series to the correct retention category.

Records Listing with Comparison Retention Periods

Figure 8-4 shows the Records Listing with both the previous and new retention periods. You will find this report valuable when you first convert to the *Skupsky Retention Method*. It shows your new and old retention periods side-by-side for comparison. You can then determine whether the differences can be justified. Expect that the new retention periods will often be different, but also expect that they should be more accurate than the old ones.

Figure 8-3. Records Retention Schedule With Records Listing

Retention Code	Retention Category Description / Cross Reference	Legal Group	Retention of Official Records				Retention of Copies	Office of Record
			Legal	User	Other	Total		
ACC1000	**Accounting** **Accounts Payable/Receivable** Records related to payment of financial obligations and receipt of revenues. Includes vouchers, vendor invoices and statements; payroll and payroll deductions; payables and revenue from customers, government contracts and grants and other sources.	ACC000	6	3	0	6	MAX1	Accounting
ACC-00-01	Accounting / Accounts Payable	accounts payable						
ACC-00-02	Accounting / Accounts Payable	accounts payable invoices						
ACC-00-04	Accounting / Accounts Payable	amortization records						
ACC-00-05	Accounting / Accounts Payable	bills						
ACC-00-06	Accounting / Accounts Payable	cash disbursements						
ACC-00-08	Accounting / Accounts Payable	cost accounting records						
ACC-00-09	Accounting / Accounts Payable	cost sheets						
ACC-00-10	Accounting / Accounts Payable	cost statements						
ACC-00-11	Accounting / Accounts Payable	credit card charge slips						
ACC-00-12	Accounting / Accounts Payable	credit card statements						
ACC-00-13	Accounting / Accounts Payable	debit advices						
ACC-00-14	Accounting / Accounts Payable	donations						
ACC-00-15	Accounting / Accounts Payable	expense reports						
ACC-00-16	Accounting / Accounts Payable	invoices						
ACC-00-17	Accounting / Accounts Payable	petty cash records						
ACC-00-18	Accounting / Accounts Payable	property taxes						
ACC-00-20	Accounting / Accounts Payable	royalty payments						
ACC-00-21	Accounting / Accounts Payable	travel expenses						
ACC-00-22	Accounting / Accounts Payable	unemployment insurance payments						
ACC-00-23	Accounting / Accounts Payable	vouchers						
ACC-00-24	Accounting / Accounts Payable	workers compensation insurance payments						
ACC-10-01	Accounting / Accounts Receivable	accounts receivable						
ACC-10-05	Accounting / Accounts Receivable	cash receipts						
ACC-10-06	Accounting / Accounts Receivable	cash sales slips						

Figure 8-4. Records Listing with Comparison Retention Periods

Department / Location Record Series	Record Code	Retention Category Code	New Retention Period	Old Retention Period	Status
Accounting					
Accounts Payable					
accounts payable	ACC-00-01	ACC1000	6	10	Official
accounts payable invoices	ACC-00-02	ACC1000	6	10	Official
accounts payable ledgers	ACC-00-03	ACC1010	10	50	Official
amortization records	ACC-00-04	ACC1000	6	50	Official
bills	ACC-00-05	ACC1000	6	3	Official
cash disbursements	ACC-00-06	ACC1000	6	6	Official
commission statements	ACC-00-07	MIS1000	1	3	Official
cost accounting records	ACC-00-08	ACC1000	6	1	Official
cost sheets	ACC-00-09	ACC1000	6	1	Official
cost statements	ACC-00-10	ACC1000	6	1	Official
credit card charge slips	ACC-00-11	ACC1000	6	3	Official
credit card statements	ACC-00-12	ACC1000	6	3	Official
debit advices	ACC-00-13	ACC1000	6	1	Official
donations	ACC-00-14	ACC1000	6	6	Official
expense reports	ACC-00-15	ACC1000	6	3	Official
invoices	ACC-00-16	ACC1000	6	10	Official
petty cash records	ACC-00-17	ACC1000	6	3	Official
property taxes	ACC-00-18	ACC1000	6	50	Official
purchase requisitions	ACC-00-19	FIN8000	3	3	Official
royalty payments	ACC-00-20	ACC1000	6	ACT+6	Official
travel expenses	ACC-00-21	ACC1000	6	3	Official
unemployment insurance payments	ACC-00-22	ACC1000	6	10	Official
vouchers	ACC-00-23	ACC1000	6	6	Official
workers compensation insurance payments	ACC-00-24	ACC1000	6	10	Official
Accounts Receivable					
accounts receivable	ACC-10-01	ACC1000	6	6	Official
accounts receivable ledgers	ACC-10-02	ACC1010	10	50	Official
cash books	ACC-10-03	ACC1010	10	50	Official
cash journals	ACC-10-04	ACC1010	10	50	Official
cash receipts	ACC-10-05	ACC1000	6	3	Official
cash sales slips	ACC-10-06	ACC1000	6	3	Official
collection notices	ACC-10-07	FIN9900	3	3	Official
collection records	ACC-10-08	FIN9900	3	3	Official
credit advices	ACC-10-09	ACC1000	6	3	Official
receipts	ACC-10-10	ACC1000	6	10	Official
sales receipts	ACC-10-11	ACC1000	6	6	Official
uncollected accounts	ACC-10-12	ACC1000	6	IND	Official
Capital Property					
acquisitions	ACC-20-01	ACC2000	ACT+6	IND	Official
capital asset records	ACC-20-02	ACC2000	ACT+6	IND	Official
depreciation schedules	ACC-20-03	ACC2000	ACT+6	IND	Official
fixed assets	ACC-20-04	ACC2000	ACT+6	IND	Official
material transfer files	ACC-20-05	ACC2000	ACT+6	10	Official
mortgage payments	ACC-20-06	ACC1000	6	IND	Official

Chapter 9   The Concluding Procedures

You have now prepared the retention information for your organization. During the concluding procedures you will establish procedures for destruction of records and prepare the records retention program procedures manual. You also will distribute the retention reports and procedures for review and obtain approval for the entire records retention program.

HOW TO PERFORM THE CONCLUDING PROCEDURES

☐ Prepare the records retention procedures manual to specify how to destroy records, how to suspend destruction of records and how to audit the program for compliance.

☐ Distribute copies of all the records retention reports including the legal research and procedures to legal counsel for review of legal issues.

☐ Distribute copies of the Records Retention Schedule, the Records Listing with Retention Periods and the procedures to all departments for the review of the nonlegal retention periods and other retention issues.

☐ Revise the retention reports and procedures based upon the comments from the reviewers.

☐ Obtain signed approval for the final program from legal counsel, tax, department heads, records management and the chief executive officer.

☐ Maintain documentation of the records retention program including program development, legal research, the records retention reports, the program reviews and revisions, the written procedures, the approvals, the audits and destruction of records.

☐ Distribute copies of the records retention manual throughout the organization.

☐ Implement, operate and maintain the records retention program.

THE PROCEDURES MANUAL

You may develop the records retention procedures either before or after the review of the Records Retention Schedule and related reports. If you develop the procedures early, they can be reviewed with the retention schedule and assist reviewers to understand the overall records retention program. If you develop the procedures afterwards, you must distribute them later for review.

The records retention procedure manual should describe the procedures identified throughout this book. Besides the procedures for creating and interpreting the records retention reports, you should create procedures that address the following:

- Program Review

- Program Revision

- Program Approval

- Program Documentation

- Suspension of Destruction

- Destruction of Records

- Audits

PROGRAM REVIEW

The review of the Records Retention Schedules and procedures can proceed simultaneously. Legal counsel will approve the legal periods and users will approve the other retention periods. All will review the procedures.

Material distributed for review should be in the final form and appear professional. Organize the review material in a looseleaf or bound form with tabs separating each section.

If you have the capabilities, typeset all the reports. Reviewers are less likely to make trivial changes to typeset materials. They will still recommend important changes if they have a good reason.

Never distribute retention materials for review in handwritten form, with cross-outs or with errors. If you do not take the review process seriously, your reviewers will not either.

Request comments from people who do not respond by the deadline. If they do not respond in a reasonable time, seek help from upper management. You need a complete review for an accurate records retention program. You may also request certain individuals to review certain sections of the retention schedules or procedures very carefully because you feel those sections require special attention.

Review of Legal Retention Periods

Provide your legal counsel with the following information for review:

- *The Explanation and Procedures.* Provide materials from the Records Retention Procedures Manual describing the retention program, the various files and reports, and the program procedures.

- *The Legal Research.* If legal counsel has access to *Legal Requirements for Business Records,* you may just need to copy unique, industry-related laws that do not appear in the state service. Otherwise, make copies of relevant laws.

- *The Legal Research Index.* You should sort the index by legal group code and then citation. Your legal counsel can quickly review those laws associated with each legal group. Some may also request the index sorted in citation or subject order to review whether you considered certain key laws.

- *The Legal Group File.* Your legal counsel should carefully review the legal requirement and legal consideration periods. The legal consideration periods, in particular, reflect your application of various legal risks and philosophies. The legal requirement periods generally represent the longest among the legal requirements. The Legal Group File documents your conclusion in these areas. If you consulted your legal counsel prior to preparing the Legal Group File, the review should proceed with only minor revision.

- *The Records Retention Schedule.* Legal counsel will review and approve the legal retention periods assigned to each retention category and the sections of the retention schedule related to legal activities. Legal counsel may also want to review other sections such as "Employment," "Environment," "Tax," and other highly regulated areas.

- *The Records Listing with Retention Periods.* This report may also prove useful during the review. By reviewing this report, Legal counsel will also become familiar with how the Records Retention Schedule relates to the organization's records.

Review of Records Retention Schedules

Select reviewers from all departments or groups in the organization. Inform them in advance when the review will start and when comments must be returned.

Provide each reviewer with the following information:

- *The Explanation and Procedures.* Provide materials from the Records Retention Procedures Manual describing the retention program, the various files and reports, and the program procedures.

- *The Records Retention Schedule.* Provide each reviewer with the entire Records Retention Schedule. You might request that some people carefully review specific sections or request the reviewers to review all applicable sections. Inform them that legal counsel will review and approve the legal retention periods.

- *The Records Listing with Retention Periods.* You can either provide the entire listing to all reviewers or to provide only the portion of the listing that applies to each department or group. Ask them to review just the sections that apply to their department or group.

PROGRAM REVISION

Review the comments before revising the retention schedules or procedures. You may find that more than one comment relates to the same problem. The appropriate revision may contain elements from several comments.

Consider each comment carefully. Reviewers generally do not make comments unless something bothered them. You may just make the appropriate change. You may also make a different change that still resolves the problem detected.

You may also elect not to accept the proposed change, either because you do not agree with the change or do not feel that a change is needed. If you do not understand the comment, request clarification from the reviewer.

See "Records Retention Program Documentation" later in this chapter.

Keep the review copies at least until you organization approves the retention program. You may write your response to each comment next to comment or on another form. Keep the more significant reviews for longer periods to demonstrate systematic development of the retention program.

Some areas may require extensive revision. After making the appropriate changes, send revised copies of the schedules and procedures to those reviewers to ensure that you made the changes correctly. This is not necessary for simple changes.

PROGRAM APPROVAL

After completing the review and revision process, prepare copies of the final Records Retention Schedules and procedures for review. The retention schedule should then be approved in writing by the tax advisor, legal counsel, records management, department or division heads, and the highest ranking company official available (preferably the chief executive officer). The president or managing partner, tax advisor, and legal counsel in small organizations can approve the retention program for the entire organization.

The formal approval shows the organization's acceptance of the program and provides the clout necessary for implementation. It also indicates that records were destroyed pursuant to a systematic policy rather than at the whim of an individual.

PROGRAM DOCUMENTATION

Records Retention Manual

Prepare the Records Retention Schedules and procedures in a simplified form and distribute it throughout the organization. Individuals cannot comply with a program they do not know about. Review the program periodically and update it to ensure that the information is current, and meets organizational needs and legal requirements.

The Records Retention Manual should only contain the Records Retention Schedule, the Records Listing with Retention Periods and the procedures. The records retention periods can consist of only the total retention period and the retention period for copies. No legal information should appear in the Records Retention Manual—this will only confuse those implementing the program.

Records Retention Program Documentation

You should maintain the full documentation of the records retention program:

- Program development,

- Legal research, Legal Research Index, and Legal Group File,

- Records Retention Schedule,

- Records Listing with Retention Periods,

- Retention program revisions,

- Written procedures,

- Reviews and approvals,

- Record of destruction, and

- Program audits.

Your legal counsel also should maintain a copy of the legal research, Legal Research Index and Legal Group File for future review and revision.

There are no specific laws that tell you how much records retention documentation to keep and how long keep it. Many court decisions indicate that this documentation is important to show a court or regulatory agency that you have established a reasonable program and implemented procedures to comply with that program. The goal is to demonstrate that you follow a records retention program and that you destroy records regularly under the program with no intent to deceive or defraud.

You should therefore keep a "reasonable" amount of documentation for a reasonable period of time. Many organizations believe that these records should be retained about ten years to create the appropriate history and appearance of propriety. Others advocate longer or shorter periods based upon their view of what constitutes a "reasonable" period.

Destruction of Records Documentation

You should complete a "Destruction of Records Form" when you destroy records. The form should specify the following information:

- Description of records,

- Dates of records,

- Retention period,

- Date destroyed, and

- Name and signature of person supervising destruction.

The "Destruction of Records Form" should be kept for the same period as other records retention program documentation. The form may be useful to document the destruction of records in court. The form will generally provide enough information to demonstrate that you appropriately destroyed records under an approved records retention program.

DESTRUCTION OF RECORDS

You can safely destroy records when the period specified in the Records Retention Schedule ends. Most organizations destroy the records for which the retention period has expired at the same time. Every January, for example, review the records to determine which can be destroyed under the retention program.

See "Destruction of Records Documentation" later in this chapter.

Prepare the "Destruction of Records Form" listing the records to be destroyed. You may not need formal approval for destruction provided that the appropriate authorities approved the records retention and you adopt the procedures for suspension of destruction described later in this chapter. You should sign and date the Destruction of Records Form indicating that you witnessed the actual destruction of records. If you transfer them to an outside service for destruction, request a signed form from the company.

Some organizations prefer to circulate a "Notice of Destruction Form" indicating the records scheduled for destruction. Record users can then determine whether there are any compelling reasons for halting the destruction process.

You should only halt destruction if litigation, government investigation or audit is pending or imminent. Other contingencies should have been considered when you determined the retention periods. You may convene the records retention committee to determine whether the stated reason to halt destruction is compelling enough and whether the retention schedule should be changed to prevent similar problems in the future.

SUSPENSION OF DESTRUCTION

See *Recordkeeping Requirements,* **Chapter 13 for details related to records destruction and litigation.**

Do not destroy relevant records that are subject to a "hold" because litigation, government investigation or audit is pending or imminent. Either segregate these records from the files or mark them in some obvious manner indicating the reason for the "hold." You should not destroy them until you formally terminate the "hold," even if the retention period is concluded. Always check with tax, legal, and other sectors of the organization before destroying these records.

Some critics have indicated that a "Notice of Destruction" or an "Authorization for Destruction Form" should be signed prior to destruction of records. They believe this protects the organization if audit, litigation, or other changed circumstances create the need to retain these records for longer periods. By requiring appropriate authorizations prior to destruction, individuals within the organization would be afforded the opportunity to halt the destruction of certain records that should be kept for longer periods of time. Similarly, this additional review process will prevent certain records from mistakenly being destroyed before their retention period expires.

These same critics also say that department managers, in particular, may not give their approval for the Records Retention Schedule if you do not afford them an additional review of the records prior to destruction. This would result in extremely long, if not permanent, retention of many records in an organization.

These arguments all have merit. The traditional solutions, however, have proven both unsuccessful and may even compromise the integrity of your retention program. Most lawyers have indicated that they cannot determine from the records listed in the Authorization for Destruction Form which records are subject to litigation, government investigation or audit. As a result, some will refuse to approve the destruction of many records for fear of making a mistake. Others will inadvertently approve the destruction of records that should be subject to a "hold." Similarly, if given a second chance, many department heads also may "block" the destruction of records for no reason at all.

See *Recordkeeping Requirements*, Chapters 1 and 13 for details about selective destruction and selective retention, and see Chapter 4 for the adverse consequences that may result from the illegal or inappropriate destruction of records. See also Chapter 1 in this book for the benefits of a records retention program.

Records must be destroyed systematically under a records retention program to protect your organization from claims of illegal or inappropriate destruction of records. Whenever individuals decide to selectively halt the destruction process by failing to approve the Authorization for Destruction Form, they selectively retain those records. Courts view selective retention—the withholding from destruction of selected records—in the same category as selective destruction—the destruction of selected records. Both can create serious problems for your organization.

Selective retention can be justified in cases of litigation, government investigation or audit. Unfortunately, the traditional requirement for signed approvals prior to all records destruction often results in selective retention based upon the "whims" or fears of individuals. Often, you do not know the reason why certain individuals want records kept after the retention period ends. Failure to destroy records at the appropriate time also will deprive your organization of the benefits of a records retention program.

Through improved procedures, you can address the needs of your organization to place "holds" on certain records plus respond to the concerns regarding illegal or inappropriate destruction. Meet regularly with lawyers, tax managers and records coordinators in each department to determine whether records are covered by audit, litigation or other changed circumstances. Create a list of records subject to each type of "hold." Mark your records and your indexes to indicate the type, reason, duration and the person responsible for ultimately removing the hold.

The traditional, Authorization for Destruction Form provides you with warning just prior to destruction.

By arranging regular meetings and placing "holds" on records, you best serve the needs of the legal and tax departments. During these meetings everyone concerned can concentrate on determining which records are subject to holds. This procedure will also provide the organization with advanced warning about records potentially subject to litigation, government investigation or audit.

Records subject to "holds" can also be separated from other records and affirmatively protected during this period. Through this process you protect records from unauthorized access or accidental destruction during this period.

The review process for the Records Retention Schedule ensures that the retention periods are accurate. When the organization formally approves the program, you have authority to destroy records after the retention periods end. No additional approval or review is necessary. By conducting regular meetings with legal, tax, departments and others in your organization, you can accurately place "holds" on records subject to litigation, government investigation or audit.

AUDITS

Periodically conduct audits to ensure that everyone follows the Records Retention Schedule and destruction procedures. Your audit department may include the records retention audit as part of its regular duties. If the retention schedule calls for the destruction of records and you have not destroyed them without a compelling reason, courts may view this as "selective retention." And, if you only destroy selected records as part of a retention program or destroy records whose retention periods have not yet ended, the courts may view this as "selective destruction." Either selective retention or selective destruction can subject the organization to substantial fines, penalties, and the loss of rights.

You can determine what changes are necessary in the retention program through periodic internal audits. Schedule additional staff training when appropriate or adopt some coercive methods to ensure compliance with the program. Some organizations restrict the purchase of new filing equipment until all appropriate records have been destroyed or transferred to the warehouse for long-term storage.

ANNUAL PROGRAM REVIEW

You should review the retention program at least once each year. Review, revise, and obtain approval for the changes just like for the initial program.

See Chapter 2 for details regarding the *Skupsky Retention Method* and the 80/20 rule.

You may revise the program during the year to respond to special problems or to previously unanticipated needs. If you used the *Skupsky Retention Method*, you will spend most of your time fine-tuning the last 20 percent of the program. The initial 80 percent of the program will need very little attention.

Appendix A　Sample Records Retention Schedule

See Chapter 7 for details about the Records Retention Schedule.

This sample Records Retention Schedule is for a small United States company doing business in Texas.

Appendix C contains the Legal Group File and Appendix D contains the Legal Research Index. Appendix E explains the abbreviations used in this appendix.

You should customize the Records Retention Schedule to meet the unique needs of your organization.

Retention Code	Retention Category Description / Cross Reference	Legal Group	Retention of Official Records				Retention of Copies	Office of Record
			Legal	User	Other	Total		
ACC1000	**Accounting Accounts Payable/Receivable** Records related to payment of financial obligations and receipt of revenues. Includes vouchers, vendor invoices and statements; payroll and payroll deductions; government contracts and grants, contributions, and other income.	ACC000	6	3	0	6	MAX1	Accounting
ACC1010	**Accounting Journals / Ledgers** Records used to transfer charges between accounts and for summarizing account information. Final, annual records only.	ACC000	6	10	0	10	MAX1	Accounting
ACC2000	**Accounting Capital Property** Includes purchase and sales of property and equipment, depreciation, improvements, etc. Includes financial obligations associated with capital expenditures, purchase of land, buildings, equipment, furnishings, motor vehicles; material transfers, work orders, additions or improvements to building or equipment, property reporting.	ACC100	ACT+6	ACT	0	ACT+6	MAX5	Accounting
ACC9900	**Accounting General** Records related to accounting records not previously covered. Includes accounting reports, control documents; system input, maintenance and changes.	NONE	0	3	0	3	MAX1	Accounting

Retention Code	Retention Category Description / Cross Reference	Legal Group	Retention of Official Records				Retention of Copies	Office of Record
			Legal	User	Other	Total		
ADM1000	**Administration Internal Services**	NONE	0	3	0	3	MAX1	Admin.
	Records related to providing internal support for company personnel including services and products. Includes material and supplies orders; postal operations, forms management, reprographics, micrographics, airline reservations, user requests and approvals, maintenance requests. See CON2000 for service contracts and leases.							
ADM1020	**Administration Planning / Forecasting**	NONE	0	ACT+1	0	ACT+1	ACT	Various
	Records related to future planning and forecasting for internal purposes. Includes annual plans, five- and ten-year strategic plans and forecasts, facility requirements, growth forecasts.							
ADM2000	**Administration Property Management**	NONE	0	3	0	3	MAX1	Property
	Records related to the movement or tracking of company property. Includes records related to the inventory and movement of vehicles, equipment, tools, materials and supplies owned, rented or leased; use logs.							
ADM2020	**Administration Property Management Construction / Maintenance**	NONE	0	ACT+3	0	ACT+3	ACT	Property
	Records related to the construction, design, maintenance and repair of company property.							

Retention Code	Retention Category Description / Cross Reference	Legal Group	Retention of Official Records				Retention of Copies	Office of Record
			Legal	User	Other	Total		
ADM3000	**Administration Policies / Procedures**	POL000	ACT+10	ACT	0	ACT+10	SUP	Various
	Records documenting company-approved procedures for performing activities to ensure uniformity and compliance with company and legal requirements. Includes office and job practices, administrative handbooks, procedures manuals, software and equipment manuals.							
ADM3010	**Administration Policies / Procedures Audits, Internal**	NONE	0	2	0	2	MAX1	Auditing
	Records demonstrating compliance with internal policies and procedures. Includes audit reports, remedial activities, and workpapers. See ADM3000 for actual policy or procedure.							
ADM3020	**Administration Policies / Procedures Compliance**	POL100	10	3	0	10	MAX3	Various
	Records related to compliance with internal policies and procedures. Includes records destruction certificates. See ADM3000 for actual policy or procedure.							
ADM4000	**Administration Security**	NONE	0	3	0	3	MAX1	Security
	Records related to protect employees, equipment, buildings and information. Includes security clearances, pass card lists, password lists.							

XYZ Company
Records Retention Schedule

Records Retention Program

Retention Code	Retention Category Description / Cross Reference	Legal Group	Retention of Official Records				Retention of Copies	Office of Record
			Legal	User	Other	Total		
ADM9900	**Administration General** Records related to administration activities not previously covered. Includes housekeeping, departmental administration, administrative reports.	NONE	0	MAX3	0	MAX3	MAX1	Various
ADM9910	**Administration General Chronological Files** Copies of records maintained as backup by authors. See the appropriate retention category for the retention period for the official records.	NONE	0	MAX1	0	MAX1	MAX1	Various
ENV1000	**Environment Testing** Records related to the testing, monitoring and analysis of the environment. Excludes hazardous substances and ground water.	ENV200	3	5	0	5	1	Testing
ENV2000	**Environment Hazardous Substances** Records related to the use, manufacture, and testing of hazardous substances.	ENV100	IND	IND	0	IND	ACT	Operations
ENV2010	**Environment Hazardous Substances Transportation** Records related to the transportation of hazardous substances. Includes shipping manifests for hazardous substances.	ENV110	3	3	0	3	MAX1	Operations

Retention Code	Retention Category Description / Cross Reference	Legal Group	Retention of Official Records				Retention of Copies	Office of Record
			Legal	User	Other	Total		
ENV3000	**Environment** **Water Pollution** Records related to testing of ground water for pollution and contamination from hazardous substances.	ENV200	3	3	0	3	MAX1	Operations
FIN1000	**Finance** **Banking** Records related to banking activities. Includes deposits, checks, statements, reconciliations, drafts, canceled checks, automatic deposit plans, check registers, cash management.	ACC000	6	3	0	6	MAX1	Finance
FIN2000	**Finance** **Budgets / Financial Forecasts** Records related to internal planning and financial management.	NONE	0	ACT+1	0	ACT+1	ACT	Finance
FIN3000	**Finance** **Investments** Records related to passive investments in stocks, bonds, mutual funds, etc. to track and management investments including pension funds. See ACC2000 for accounting for investments.	ACC100	ACT+6	ACT+3	0	ACT+6	SUP	Finance
FIN4000	**Finance** **Bonds / Debentures** Records related to company's issuance of debt and equity papers. Includes bonds and debenture ledgers, certificate transfers, notes receivables, sinking funds. See CON2000 for actual bonds (contracts).	ACC100	ACT+6	ACT+3	0	ACT+6	MAX1	Finance

Retention Code	Retention Category Description / Cross Reference	Legal Group	Retention of Official Records				Retention of Copies	Office of Record
			Legal	User	Other	Total		
FIN5000	**Finance Loans / Credits** Records related to the applications, issuance, management and administration of loans to the company. Includes correspondence with lenders, reports to lenders, debt information, work papers, writeoffs, write downs, losses.	ACC100	ACT+6	ACT+3	0	ACT+6	MAX3	Finance
FIN6000	**Finance Bad Debts** Records related to the monitoring, collecting and writing off of bad debts. Includes authorizations, supporting details of uncollectible accounts.	ACC000	6	3	0	6	MAX1	Finance
FIN7000	**Finance Financial Statements** Financial statements, reports, and background information submitted to government agencies, shareholders, partners, etc. Includes financial statements submitted to SEC, IRS, states, etc.	BUS130	10	10	0	10	MAX1	Finance
FIN8000	**Finance Purchasing** Records related to request for bids, bid review, receiving, inspection of merchandise, etc. See ACC1000 for accounting for actual purchases. See LEG2000 for purchasing contracts.	NONE	0	3	0	3	MAX1	Finance
FIN9900	**Finance General** Records related to finance activities not covered previously. See ACC1000 for accounting.	NONE	0	3	0	3	MAX3	Finance

Retention Code	Retention Category Description / Cross Reference	Legal Group	Retention of Official Records				Retention of Copies	Office of Record
			Legal	User	Other	Total		
HUM1010	**Human Resources** **Benefits** **Benefit Plans**	EMP110	ACT+6	ACT+1	0	ACT+6	ACT	Benefits
	Records related to company sponsored benefit plans. Includes insurance, pension, disability, medical, survivor programs, ESOP, PAYSOP, vesting criteria, vacation entitlements, educational assistance, savings plans, correspondence explaining benefit plans. See LEG5000 for pension reports to the government.							
HUM1020	**Human Resources** **Benefits** **Contributions / Benefits Provided**	EMP100	6	3	0	6	MAX1	Benefits
	Records related to contribution and participation in company sponsored benefit plans. Includes insurance, pension, disability, savings, etc.							
HUM1030	**Human Resources** **Benefits** **Elections**	EMP100	6	ACT	0	ACT+6	MAX1	Benefits
	Records of elections by employees for type and amount of participation in company benefit plans.							
HUM1040	**Human Resources** **Benefits** **Pension Summary Information**	EMP120	6	ACT	0	ACT+6	MAX1	Benefits
	Records related to cumulative years of service, total pension contributions, accrued benefits, etc.							

Retention Code	Retention Category Description / Cross Reference	Legal Group	Retention of Official Records				Retention of Copies	Office of Record
			Legal	User	Other	Total		
HUM2000	**Human Resources Employee Selection** Records of general nature related to personnel requests, job applications, testing, advertising, interviews, etc.	EMP900	1	3	0	3	MAX1	Personnel
HUM3000	**Human Resources Employee Records Summary Records** Summary records for individual employees.	EMP300	3	ACT+3	0	ACT+3	SUP	Personnel
HUM3010	**Human Resources Employee Records Detailed Records** Records regarding specific employees. Includes hiring, promotion, performance appraisals, transfers, termination.	EMP300	3	3	0	3	MAX1	Personnel
HUM4010	**Human Resources Health and Safety Medical Records - General** Medical records related to treatment, examinations, history, etc. related to general medical matters. See HUM4020 for accident and injury reports. See HUM4030 for hazardous exposure.	EMP700	CY+5	3	0	CY+5	MAX1	Safety
HUM4020	**Human Resources Health and Safety Accidents / Injuries** Records related to on-the-job accidents often used for workers' compensation claims.	EMP700	CY+5	3	0	CY+5	MAX1	Safety

Retention Code	Retention Category Description / Cross Reference	Legal Group	Retention of Official Records				Retention of Copies	Office of Record
			Legal	User	Other	Total		
HUM40030	**Human Resources** **Health and Safety** **Hazardous Exposure** Medical records related to exposure or possible exposure to hazardous or toxic substances including testing. See ENV2000 for testing for exposure to hazardous substances.	EMP500	ACT+30	ACT	0	ACT+30	MAX1	Safety
HUM40031	**Human Resources** **Health and Safety** **Material Safety Data Sheets** Material safety data sheets required by OSHA.	ENV100	IND	3	0	IND	ACT	Safety
HUM40032	**Human Resources** **Health and Safety** **Noise Exposure** Records related to the measuring, testing and analyzing noise in the work environment.	EMP510	2	1	0	2	MAX1	Safety
HUM40033	**Human Resources** **Health and Safety** **Audiometric Testing** Records related to audiometric testing conducted for employees.	EMP511	ACT	1	0	ACT+1	MAX1	Safety

Retention Code	Retention Category Description / Cross Reference	Legal Group	Retention of Official Records				Retention of Copies	Office of Record
			Legal	User	Other	Total		
HUM5000	**Human Resources Training / Development**	EMP000	3	ACT	0	ACT+3	ACT	Training
	Records related to the development and operation of company-sponsored training programs and seminars. Includes seminars, education assistance, management and supervision development, job progression, drug and alcohol awareness, course listings, schedules, requests and approvals.							
HUM5010	**Human Resources Training and Development Certification**	EMP000	3	ACT	0	ACT+3	ACT	Training
	Records related to certification for individuals to perform certain task. Includes CPA, bar admissions, CLE, etc.							
HUM6000	**Human Resources Salary Administration**	EMP300	3	3	0	3	MAX1	Personnel
	Records related to determining and monitoring salary and deduction amounts including timesheets. See ACC1000 for accounting records for payroll and deductions.							
HUM9900	**Human Resources General**	EMP000	3	3	0	3	MAX1	Various
	Records related to salary studies and other personnel or human resources activities not covered elsewhere.							
LEG1000	**Legal Business Organization**	BUS000	IND	10	0	IND	MAX1	Executive
	Records related to the creation and formal proceedings of company including subsidiaries. See LEG2000 for partnership agreements.							

Retention Code	Retention Category Description / Cross Reference	Legal Group	Retention of Official Records				Retention of Copies	Office of Record
			Legal	User	Other	Total		
LEG1010	**Legal** **Business Organization** **Meetings** Records related to board, shareholder, and other legally-required meetings.	BUS120	10	3	0	10	MAX3	Executive
LEG1020	**Legal** **Business Organization** **Ownership** Records related to ownership of business organization. Includes stock transactions, sales of ownership rights, etc. See LEG2000 for partnership agreements.	CON000	ACT+6	ACT	0	ACT+6	ACT	Executive
LEG1030	**Legal** **Business Organization** **Former Entities** Records related to the creation and formal proceedings of defunct entities.	BUS120	10	3	0	10	MAX3	Executive
LEG2000	**Legal** **Contracts / Agreements** Records related to obligations under contracts, leases, and other agreements between company and outside parties. Includes contracts for services, purchases and sales, transportation, leases, exchange of property, and government contracts. See LEG2100 for contracts for improvements to real property.	CON000	ACT+6	ACT+1	0	ACT+6	ACT	Various

Retention Code	Retention Category Description / Cross Reference	Legal Group	Retention of Official Records				Retention of Copies	Office of Record
			Legal	User	Other	Total		
LEG2010	**Legal** **Contracts / Agreements** **Contract Performance** Records related to compliance or performance of contracts. Includes determination of costs, performance of services, payments, and work products for government contracts. See LEG2110 for compliance with contracts for improvement to real property.	CON010	6	3	0	6	MAX3	Various
LEG2100	**Legal** **Contracts - Real Property** **Improvements** Records related to contracts and agreements for improvements to real property. See LEG2000 for other contracts.	CON300	ACT+12	ACT+1	0	ACT+12	ACT	Various
LEG2110	**Legal** **Contracts - Real Property** **Improvements - Compliance** Records related to compliance under contracts for improvements to real property. See LEG2010 for compliance with other contracts.	CON310	12	3	0	12	MAX3	Various
LEG3000	**Legal** **Insurance** Records related to coverage affecting company liability. Includes policies, amendments, riders, proof of payment, etc. See HUM1010 for employee medical and life insurance.	CON000	ACT+6	ACT+1	0	ACT+6	ACT	Insurance

XYZ Company
Records Retention Schedule

Records Retention Program

Retention Code	Retention Category Description / Cross Reference	Legal Group	Retention of Official Records				Retention of Copies	Office of Record
			Legal	User	Other	Total		
LEG3010	**Legal** **Insurance** **Future Liability**	CON200	IND	IND	0	IND	ACT	Insurance
	Records related to insurance coverage for product liability, exposure to hazardous substances, or other problems manifesting themselves long after the policy terminates. Includes liability policies.							
LEG4000	**Legal** **Claims / Litigation**	LIT000	ACT+6	ACT+1	0	ACT+6	ACT	Legal
	Records related to threatened or asserted litigation or government investigation. Includes pleadings, discovery, attorney work-products, legal opinions, transcripts, exhibits, final judgments, etc.							
LEG5000	**Legal** **Compliance**	LEG000	6	6	0	6	MAX1	Legal
	Records related to the preparation of documents required by law. Includes reporting and filings with agencies such as IRS, SEC, DOT, OSHA, EPA, EEOC; external audits required by government agencies, etc. See LEG5010 for tax returns.							
LEG5010	**Legal** **Compliance** **Tax Returns**	LEG000	6	10	0	10	MAX3	Legal
	Tax returns filed for sales, income, severance, etc. See ACC1000 for detailed accounting records.							

Legal Compliance

XYZ Company
Records Retention Schedule

Records Retention Program

Retention Code	Retention Category Description / Cross Reference	Legal Group	Retention of Official Records				Retention of Copies	Office of Record
			Legal	User	Other	Total		
LEG5020	**Legal Compliance License / Permits**	LEG100	ACT+3	ACT	0	ACT+3	ACT	Legal
	Records including licenses required to conduct business, collect taxes, etc.							
LEG5030	**Legal Compliance Orders - Agency / Court**	LEG100	ACT+3	ACT	0	ACT+3	MAX3	Legal
	Records related to unique orders issued to company							
LEG6000	**Legal Legal Projects**	NONE	0	ACT+10	0	ACT+10	ACT	Legal
	Records related to providing determining legal requirements and providing legal advise within company.							
LEG6010	**Legal Legal Projects Legal Opinions**	POL000	ACT+10	IND	0	IND	ACT	Legal
	Records resulting from legal projects which document the specific legal advise provided.							
LEG7000	**Legal Copyright / Trademark / Patents**	LIT000	ACT+6	ACT+1	0	ACT+6	ACT	Legal
	Records related to preparation, filing, maintenance, and rights.							
LEG9900	**Legal General**	NONE	0	3	0	3	MAX3	Various
	Records related to legal activities not covered elsewhere.							

| Retention Code | Retention Category Description / Cross Reference | Legal Group | Retention of Official Records | | | | Retention of Copies | Office of Record |
			Legal	User	Other	Total		
MAN1000	**Manufacturing Design / Development**	MAN000	IND	ACT+5	0	IND	ACT	Operations
	Records related to the design and development of products for manufacturing.							
MAN2000	**Manufacturing Production**	MAN000	IND	ACT+5	0	IND	ACT	Operations
	Records related to production including quality control and testing.							
MAN3000	**Manufacturing Manufacturing Methods**	POL000	ACT+10	ACT+5	0	ACT+10	ACT	Operations
	Records related to manufacturing equipment or developments of manufacturing processes.							
MAN9900	**Manufacturing General**	NONE	0	MAX3	0	MAX3	MAX1	Operations
	Records of a general nature related to categories not previously covered.							
MIS0000	**Miscellaneous**	NONE	0	1	0	1	MAX1	Various
	Miscellaneous records not falling into other categories							
MIS1000	**Miscellaneous Reports / Copies**	NONE	0	1	0	1	MAX1	Various
	Miscellaneous reports and other records which need only be reviewed for a short period - day, week, quarter, current year.							

Miscellaneous Reports / Copies

XYZ Company
Records Retention Schedule

Records Retention Program

Retention Code	Retention Category Description / Cross Reference	Legal Group	Retention of Official Records				Retention of Copies	Office of Record
			Legal	User	Other	Total		
MIS1010	**Miscellaneous Reports / Copies Periodic Replacement Records** Records replaced periodically by newer, updated ones.	NONE	0	SUP	0	SUP	MAX3	Various
MIS1020	**Miscellaneous Reports / Copies Transmittal Forms** Records used to transmit information to another record.	NONE	0	1M	0	1M	1M	Various
MIS2000	**Miscellaneous Special Projects** Records related to special projects that do not fall into any other category.	NONE	0	ACT+1	0	ACT+1	ACT	Various
PUB1000	**Public Affairs Community Relations** Records related to participation or promotion of company activities, associations, charitable contributions, civic organizations, etc.	NONE	0	3	0	3	MAX1	Executive
PUB2000	**Public Affairs Government Relations** Records related to monitoring government activities, proposed laws and political action committees.	NONE	0	5	0	5	MAX1	Legal
PUB3000	**Public Affairs Publicity** Records related to marketing and promoting company image and activities such as press releases, publications, photographs.	NONE	0	5	0	5	MAX1	Sales

Retention Code	Retention Category Description / Cross Reference	Legal Group	Retention of Official Records				Retention of Copies	Office of Record
			Legal	User	Other	Total		
PUB4000	**Public Affairs Employee Relations** Records related to informative communications to employees such as newsletters, letters from management, etc.	NONE	0	3	0	3	MAX1	Personnel
PUB5000	**Public Affairs Industry Relations** Records related to information on other industries and companies.	NONE	0	ACT	0	ACT	ACT	Executive
PUB6000	**Public Affairs Publications** Publications produced by company.Library maintain one copy of all completed publications for reference purposes.	NONE	0	5	0	5	MAX1	Various
PUB9900	**Public Affairs General** Records related to public affairs not covered elsewhere.	NONE	0	3	0	3	MAX1	Various
REF0000	**Reference** Records and non-record material maintained for reference purposes only.	NONE	0	SUP	0	SUP	SUP	Various
SAL1000	**Sales Advertising / Marketing** Records related to advertising and claims made to potential clients. Includes brochures, bids, proposals, etc.	ADV000	ACT+2	3	0	ACT+3	MAX1	Sales

Appendix B

Sample Records Listing With Retention Periods

See Chapter 8 for details about the Records Listing with Records Retention Periods. The record series were taken from *Recordkeeping Requirements*, Chapter 12.

This sample Records Listing With Retention Periods is for a small United States company doing business in Texas.

Appendix A contains the Records Retention Schedule used to determine the retention periods, Appendix C contains the Legal Group File and Appendix D contains the Legal Research Index. Appendix E explains the abbreviations used in this appendix.

You should customize the Records Listing With Retention Periods to meet the unique needs of your organization.

XYZ Company
Records Listing With Retention Periods

Records Retention Program

Department / Location Record Series	Record Code	Retention Category	Legal Group	Retention of Official Records				Retention of Copies	Office of Record	Status
				Legal	User	Other	Total			

Accounting

Accounts Payable

Department / Location Record Series	Record Code	Retention Category	Legal Group	Legal	User	Other	Total	Retention of Copies	Office of Record	Status
accounts payable	ACC-00-01	ACC1000	ACC000	6	3	0	6	MAX1	Accounting	Official
accounts payable invoices	ACC-00-02	ACC1000	ACC000	6	3	0	6	MAX1	Accounting	Official
accounts payable ledgers	ACC-00-03	ACC1010	ACC000	6	10	0	10	MAX1	Accounting	Official
amortization records	ACC-00-04	ACC1000	ACC000	6	3	0	6	MAX1	Accounting	Official
bills	ACC-00-05	ACC1000	ACC000	6	3	0	6	MAX1	Accounting	Official
cash disbursements	ACC-00-06	ACC1000	ACC000	6	3	0	6	MAX1	Accounting	Official
commission statements	ACC-00-07	MIS1000	NONE	0	1	0	1	MAX1	Various	Official
cost accounting records	ACC-00-08	ACC1000	ACC000	6	3	0	6	MAX1	Accounting	Official
cost sheets	ACC-00-09	ACC1000	ACC000	6	3	0	6	MAX1	Accounting	Official
cost statements	ACC-00-10	ACC1000	ACC000	6	3	0	6	MAX1	Accounting	Official
credit card charge slips	ACC-00-11	ACC1000	ACC000	6	3	0	6	MAX1	Accounting	Official
credit card statements	ACC-00-12	ACC1000	ACC000	6	3	0	6	MAX1	Accounting	Official
debit advices	ACC-00-13	ACC1000	ACC000	6	3	0	6	MAX1	Accounting	Official
donations	ACC-00-14	ACC1000	ACC000	6	3	0	6	MAX1	Accounting	Official
expense reports	ACC-00-15	ACC1000	ACC000	6	3	0	6	MAX1	Accounting	Official
invoices	ACC-00-16	ACC1000	ACC000	6	3	0	6	MAX1	Accounting	Official
petty cash records	ACC-00-17	ACC1000	ACC000	6	3	0	6	MAX1	Accounting	Official
property taxes	ACC-00-18	ACC1000	ACC000	6	3	0	6	MAX1	Accounting	Official
purchase requisitions	ACC-00-19	FIN8000	NONE	0	3	0	3	MAX1	Finance	Official
royalty payments	ACC-00-20	ACC1000	ACC000	6	3	0	6	MAX1	Accounting	Official
travel expenses	ACC-00-21	ACC1000	ACC000	6	3	0	6	MAX1	Accounting	Official
unemployment insurance payments	ACC-00-22	ACC1000	ACC000	6	3	0	6	MAX1	Accounting	Official
vouchers	ACC-00-23	ACC1000	ACC000	6	3	0	6	MAX1	Accounting	Official
workers compensation insurance payments	ACC-00-24	ACC1000	ACC000	6	3	0	6	MAX1	Accounting	Official
Accounts Receivable										
accounts receivable	ACC-10-01	ACC1000	ACC000	6	3	0	6	MAX1	Accounting	Official
accounts receivable ledgers	ACC-10-02	ACC1010	ACC000	6	10	0	10	MAX1	Accounting	Official
cash books	ACC-10-03	ACC1010	ACC000	6	10	0	10	MAX1	Accounting	Official

XYZ Company
Records Listing With Retention Periods

Accounting (continued)

Department/Location Record Series	Record Code	Retention Category	Legal Group	Retention of Official Records				Retention of Copies	Office of Record	Status
				Legal	User	Other	Total			
Accounts Receivable (continued)										
cash journals	ACC-10-04	ACC1010	ACC000	6	10	0	10	MAX1	Accounting	Official
cash receipts	ACC-10-05	ACC1000	ACC000	6	10	0	10	MAX1	Accounting	Official
cash sales slips	ACC-10-06	ACC1000	ACC000	6	3	0	6	MAX1	Accounting	Official
collection notices	ACC-10-07	FIN9900	NONE	0	3	0	3	MAX3	Finance	Official
collection records	ACC-10-08	FIN9900	NONE	0	3	0	3	MAX3	Finance	Official
credit advices	ACC-10-09	ACC1000	ACC000	6	3	0	6	MAX1	Accounting	Official
receipts	ACC-10-10	ACC1000	ACC000	6	3	0	6	MAX1	Accounting	Official
sales receipts	ACC-10-11	ACC1000	ACC000	6	3	0	6	MAX1	Accounting	Official
uncollected accounts	ACC-10-12	ACC1000	ACC000	6	3	0	6	MAX1	Accounting	Official
Capital Property										
acquisitions	ACC-20-01	ACC2000	ACC100	ACT+6	ACT	0	ACT+6	MAX5	Accounting	Official
capital asset records	ACC-20-02	ACC2000	ACC100	ACT+6	ACT	0	ACT+6	MAX5	Accounting	Official
depreciation schedules	ACC-20-03	ACC2000	ACC100	ACT+6	ACT	0	ACT+6	MAX5	Accounting	Official
fixed assets	ACC-20-04	ACC2000	ACC100	ACT+6	ACT	0	ACT+6	MAX5	Accounting	Official
material transfer files	ACC-20-05	ACC2000	ACC100	ACT+6	ACT	0	ACT+6	MAX5	Accounting	Official
mortgage payments	ACC-20-06	ACC1000	ACC000	6	3	0	6	MAX1	Accounting	Official
plant ledgers	ACC-20-07	ACC2000	ACC100	ACT+6	ACT	0	ACT+6	MAX5	Accounting	Official
property detail records	ACC-20-08	ACC2000	ACC100	ACT+6	ACT	0	ACT+6	MAX5	Accounting	Official
property inventory	ACC-20-09	ACC2000	ACC100	ACT+6	ACT	0	ACT+6	MAX5	Accounting	Official
property, sold	ACC-20-10	ACC1000	ACC000	6	3	0	6	MAX1	Accounting	Official
General										
account ledgers	ACC-30-01	ACC1010	ACC000	6	10	0	10	MAX1	Accounting	Official
accounting procedures	ACC-30-02	ADM3000	POL000	ACT+10	ACT	0	ACT+10	SUP	Various	Official
books of accounts	ACC-30-03	ACC1000	ACC000	6	3	0	6	MAX1	Accounting	Official
credit applications	ACC-30-04	FIN9900	NONE	0	3	0	3	MAX3	Finance	Official
general ledger, annual	ACC-30-05	ACC1010	ACC000	6	10	0	10	MAX1	Accounting	Official
general ledger, monthly	ACC-30-06	MIS1000	NONE	0	1	0	1	MAX1	Various	Official

Accounting (continued)

Department / Location Record Series	Record Code	Retention Category	Legal Group	Retention of Official Records				Retention of Copies	Office of Record	Status
				Legal	User	Other	Total	Total of Copies		
General (continued)										
journal entries	ACC-30-07	ACC1010	ACC000			0	1	MAX1	Various	Official
journals	ACC-30-08	ACC1010	ACC000	6	10	0	10	MAX1	Accounting	Official
ledgers	ACC-30-09	ACC1010	ACC000	6	10	0	10	MAX1	Accounting	Official
ledgers, subsidiary	ACC-30-10	ACC1010	ACC000	6	10	0	10	MAX1	Accounting	Official
registers	ACC-30-11	ACC1010	ACC000	6	10	0	10	MAX1	Accounting	Official
trial balances	ACC-30-12	ACC1010	ACC000	6	10	0	10	MAX1	Accounting	Official
Payroll										
garnishment accounting	ACC-40-01	ACC1000	ACC000	6	3	0	6	MAX1	Accounting	Official
garnishment orders	ACC-40-02	LEG5030	LEG100	ACT+3	ACT	0	ACT+3	MAX3	Legal	Official
payroll checks	ACC-40-03	FIN1000	ACC000	6	3	0	6	MAX1	Finance	Official
payroll history	ACC-40-04	ACC1000	ACC000	6	3	0	6	MAX1	Accounting	Official
payroll records	ACC-40-05	ACC1000	ACC000	6	3	0	6	MAX1	Accounting	Official
payroll registers	ACC-40-06	ACC1010	ACC000	6	10	0	10	MAX1	Accounting	Official

Administration

Department / Location Record Series	Record Code	Retention Category	Legal Group	Retention of Official Records				Retention of Copies	Office of Record	Status
				Legal	User	Other	Total	Total of Copies		
General										
authorizations, table of	ADM-00-01	ADM3000	POL000	ACT+10	ACT	0	ACT+10	SUP	Various	Official
calendar books	ADM-00-02	ADM9900	NONE	0	MAX3	0	MAX3	MAX1	Various	Official
chronological files	ADM-00-03	ADM9910	NONE	0	MAX1	0	MAX1	MAX1	Various	Official
correspondence (see specific listing)	ADM-00-04	ADM9900	NONE	0	MAX3	0	MAX3	MAX1	Various	Official
directives	ADM-00-05	ADM3000	POL000	ACT+10	ACT	0	ACT+10	SUP	Various	Official
feasibility studies	ADM-00-06	ADM1020	NONE	0	ACT+1	0	ACT+1	ACT	Various	Official
organization charts	ADM-00-07	ADM9900	NONE	0	MAX3	0	MAX3	MAX1	Various	Official
policies	ADM-00-08	ADM3000	POL000	ACT+10	ACT	0	ACT+10	SUP	Various	Official
policy statements	ADM-00-09	ADM3000	POL000	ACT+10	ACT	0	ACT+10	SUP	Various	Official
procedure manuals	ADM-00-10	ADM3000	POL000	ACT+10	ACT	0	ACT+10	SUP	Various	Official
reading files	ADM-00-11	ADM9910	NONE	0	MAX1	0	MAX1	MAX1	Various	Official

XYZ Company
Records Listing With Retention Periods

Administration (continued)

Department / Location Record Series	Record Code	Retention Category	Legal Group	Retention of Official Records — Legal	User	Other	Total	Retention of Copies	Office of Record	Status
General (continued)										
table of authorizations	ADM-00-12	ADM3000	POL000	ACT+10	ACT	0	ACT+10	SUP	Various	Official
telephone calls	ADM-00-13	ADM9910	NONE	0	MAX1	0	MAX1	MAX1	Various	Official
Property / Facilities										
building permits	ADM-10-01	LEG5020	LEG100	ACT+3	ACT	0	ACT+3	ACT	Legal	Official
deeds	ADM-10-02	LEG2000	CON000	ACT+6	ACT+1	0	ACT+6	ACT	Various	Official
lease abstracts	ADM-10-03	LEG2000	CON000	ACT+6	ACT+1	0	ACT+6	ACT	Various	Official
lmaintenance records	ADM-10-05	ADM2020	NONE	0	ACT+3	0	ACT+3	ACT	Property	Official
motor vehicle maintenance records	ADM-10-06	ADM2020	NONE	0	ACT+3	0	ACT+3	ACT	Property	Official
motor vehicle records	ADM-10-07	ADM2020	NONE	0	ACT+3	0	ACT+3	ACT	Property	Official
office improvements	ADM-10-08	ADM2020	NONE	0	ACT+3	0	ACT+3	ACT	Property	Official
office layout	ADM-10-09	ADM2020	NONE	0	ACT+3	0	ACT+3	ACT	Property	Official
property summaries	ADM-10-10	ACC2000	ACC100	ACT+6	ACT	0	ACT+6	MAX5	Accounting	Official
property title	ADM-10-11	LEG2000	CON000	ACT+6	ACT+1	0	ACT+6	ACT	Various	Official
real estate records	ADM-10-12	ADM2020	NONE	0	ACT+3	0	ACT+3	ACT	Property	Official
repair records	ADM-10-13	ADM2020	NONE	0	ACT+3	0	ACT+3	ACT	Property	Official
water rights	ADM-10-14	LEG2000	CON000	ACT+6	ACT+1	0	ACT+6	ACT	Various	Official
zoning permits	ADM-10-15	LEG5020	LEG100	ACT+3	ACT	0	ACT+3	ACT	Legal	Official
Records Management										
computer tape indexes	ADM-20-01	REF0000	NONE	0	SUP	0	SUP	SUP	Various	Official
forms management records	ADM-20-02	REF0000	NONE	0	SUP	0	SUP	SUP	Various	Official
record destruction records	ADM-20-03	ADM3020	POL100	10	3	0	10	MAX3	Various	Official
records inventory	ADM-20-04	MIS2000	NONE	0	ACT+1	0	ACT+1	ACT	Various	Official
Security										
badge lists	ADM-30-01	ADM4000	NONE	0	3	0	3	MAX1	Security	Official
employee clearance listings	ADM-30-02	ADM4000	NONE	0	3	0	3	MAX1	Security	Official
visitor registration	ADM-30-03	ADM4000	NONE	0	3	0	3	MAX1	Security	Official

Business Organization

Corporation

Department / Location Record Series	Record Code	Retention Category	Legal Group	Retention of Official Records			Retention of Copies	Office of Record	Status
				Legal	User Other	Total			
S.E.C. filing	BUS-00-01	LEG5000	LEG000	6	6	0	6	MAX1	Legal	Official
annual reports	BUS-00-02	FIN7000	BUS130	10	10	0	10	MAX1	Finance	Official
articles of incorporation	BUS-00-03	LEG1000	BUS000	IND	10	0	IND	MAX1	Executive	Official
board of directors meeting minutes	BUS-00-04	LEG1010	BUS120	10	3	0	10	MAX3	Executive	Official
board of directors meeting notices	BUS-00-05	LEG1010	BUS120	10	3	0	10	MAX3	Executive	Official
bonds, surety	BUS-00-06	LEG2000	CON000	ACT+6	ACT+1	0	ACT+6	ACT	Various	Official
bylaws	BUS-00-07	ADM3000	POL000	ACT+10	ACT	0	ACT+10	SUP	Various	Official
capital stock certificates	BUS-00-08	LEG1020	CON000	ACT+6	ACT	0	ACT+6	ACT	Executive	Official
capital stock ledgers	BUS-00-09	LEG1020	CON000	ACT+6	ACT	0	ACT+6	ACT	Executive	Official
capital stock records	BUS-00-10	LEG1020	CON000	ACT+6	ACT	0	ACT+6	ACT	Executive	Official
capital stock sales	BUS-00-11	ACC1000	ACC000	6	3	0	6	MAX1	Accounting	Official
capital stock transfers	BUS-00-12	LEG2010	CON010	6	3	0	6	MAX3	Various	Official
certificates of incorporation	BUS-00-13	LEG1000	BUS000	IND	10	0	IND	MAX1	Executive	Official
corporate reorganizations	BUS-00-14	LEG1020	CON000	ACT+6	ACT	0	ACT+6	ACT	Executive	Official
dividend records	BUS-00-15	ACC1000	ACC000	6	3	0	6	MAX1	Accounting	Official
fidelity bonds	BUS-00-16	LEG3000	CON000	ACT+6	ACT+1	0	ACT+6	ACT	Insurance	Official
incorporation records	BUS-00-17	LEG1000	BUS000	IND	10	0	IND	MAX1	Executive	Official
minute books	BUS-00-18	LEG1010	BUS120	10	3	0	10	MAX3	Executive	Official
proxies, signed	BUS-00-19	LEG1010	BUS120	10	3	0	10	MAX3	Executive	Official
shareholder meeting minutes	BUS-00-20	LEG1010	BUS120	10	3	0	10	MAX3	Executive	Official
shareholder meeting notices	BUS-00-21	LEG1010	BUS120	10	3	0	10	MAX3	Executive	Official
shareholder proxies	BUS-00-22	LEG1010	BUS120	10	3	0	10	MAX3	Executive	Official
stock ledgers	BUS-00-23	LEG1020	CON000	ACT+6	ACT	0	ACT+6	ACT	Executive	Official
stockholders meetings	BUS-00-24	LEG1010	BUS120	10	3	0	10	MAX3	Executive	Official
stockholders proxies	BUS-00-25	LEG1010	BUS120	10	3	0	10	MAX3	Executive	Official
stockholders, listing of	BUS-00-26	LEG1020	CON000	ACT+6	ACT	0	ACT+6	ACT	Executive	Official
voting records	BUS-00-27	LEG1010	BUS120	10	3	0	10	MAX3	Executive	Official

Business Organization (continued)

Department / Location Record Series	Record Code	Retention Category	Legal Group	Retention of Official Records			Retention of Copies	Office of Record	Status
				Legal	User Other	Total			
General									
business permits	BUS-10-01	LEG5020	LEG100	ACT+3	ACT	0	ACT+3	ACT	Legal	Official
charters	BUS-10-02	LEG5020	LEG100	ACT+3	ACT	0	ACT+3	ACT	Legal	Official
licenses	BUS-10-03	LEG5020	LEG100	ACT+3	ACT	0	ACT+3	ACT	Legal	Official
mergers	BUS-10-04	LEG2000	CON000	ACT+6	ACT+1	0	ACT+6	ACT	Various	Official
quarterly reports	BUS-10-05	MIS1000	NONE	0	1	0	1	MAX1	Various	Official
Partnership									
partnership agreements	BUS-20-01	LEG2000	CON000	ACT+6	ACT+1	0	ACT+6	ACT	Various	Official

Finance

Department / Location Record Series	Record Code	Retention Category	Legal Group	Retention of Official Records			Retention of Copies	Office of Record	Status
				Legal	User Other	Total			
Banking									
bank deposits	FIN-00-01	FIN1000	ACC000	6	3	0	6	MAX1	Finance	Official
bank reconciliations	FIN-00-02	FIN1000	ACC000	6	3	0	6	MAX1	Finance	Official
bank statements	FIN-00-03	FIN1000	ACC000	6	3	0	6	MAX1	Finance	Official
check registers	FIN-00-04	FIN1000	ACC000	6	3	0	6	MAX1	Finance	Official
check stubs	FIN-00-05	FIN1000	ACC000	6	3	0	6	MAX1	Finance	Official
checks, canceled	FIN-00-06	FIN1000	ACC000	6	3	0	6	MAX1	Finance	Official
deposit slips	FIN-00-07	FIN1000	ACC000	6	3	0	6	MAX1	Finance	Official
wire transfers	FIN-00-08	FIN1000	ACC000	6	3	0	6	MAX1	Finance	Official
General									
audit reports, external	FIN-10-01	FIN7000	BUS130	10	10	0	10	MAX1	Finance	Official
audit reports, internal	FIN-10-02	ADM3010	NONE	0	2	0	2	MAX1	Auditing	Official
balance sheets	FIN-10-03	ACC1010	ACC000	6	10	0	10	MAX1	Accounting	Official
budget workpapers	FIN-10-04	FIN2000	NONE	0	ACT+1	0	ACT+1	ACT	Finance	Official
budgets - 1 year	FIN-10-05	FIN2000	NONE	0	ACT+1	0	ACT+1	ACT	Finance	Official
budgets - 5 year	FIN-10-06	FIN2000	NONE	0	ACT+1	0	ACT+1	ACT	Finance	Official
financial plan	FIN-10-07	FIN2000	NONE	0	ACT+1	0	ACT+1	ACT	Finance	Official
financial reports - annual	FIN-10-08	FIN7000	BUS130	10	10	0	10	MAX1	Finance	Official

XYZ Company
Records Listing With Retention Periods

Finance (continued)

Department / Location Record Series	Record Code	Retention Category	Legal Group	Retention of Official Records				Retention of Copies	Office of Record	Status
				Legal	User	Other	Total			
General (continued)										
financial reports - monthly	FIN-10-09	MIS1000	NONE	0	0	0	1	MAX1	Various	Official
financial statements	FIN-10-10	FIN7000	BUS130	10	10	0	10	MAX1	Finance	Official
financial statements, certified	FIN-10-11	FIN7000	BUS130	10	10	0	10	MAX1	Finance	Official
forecasts - 1 year	FIN-10-12	FIN2000	NONE	0	ACT+1	0	ACT+1	ACT	Finance	Official
forecasts - 5 year	FIN-10-13	FIN2000	NONE	0	ACT+1	0	ACT+1	ACT	Finance	Official
profit and loss statements	FIN-10-14	FIN7000	BUS130	10	10	0	10	MAX1	Finance	Official
Investments / Insurance										
bond investments	FIN-20-01	FIN3000	ACC100	ACT+6	ACT+3	0	ACT+6	SUP	Finance	Official
futures investments	FIN-20-02	FIN3000	ACC100	ACT+6	ACT+3	0	ACT+6	SUP	Finance	Official
insurance policies, active	FIN-20-03	LEG3000	CON000	ACT+6	ACT+1	0	ACT+6	ACT	Insurance	Official
insurance policies, canceled	FIN-20-04	LEG2010	CON010	6	3	0	6	MAX3	Various	Official
inventory, property	FIN-20-05	ACC2000	ACC100	ACT+6	ACT	0	ACT+6	SUP	Accounting	Official
investments	FIN-20-06	FIN3000	ACC100	ACT+6	ACT+3	0	ACT+6	SUP	Finance	Official
letters f credit	FIN-20-07	FIN5000	ACC100	ACT+6	ACT+3	0	ACT+6	MAX3	Finance	Official
mortgage records	FIN-20-08	LEG2000	CON000	ACT+6	ACT+1	0	ACT+6	ACT	Various	Official
notes, canceled	FIN-20-09	LEG2010	CON010	6	3	0	6	MAX3	Various	Official
notes, outstanding	FIN-20-10	LEG2000	CON000	ACT+6	ACT+1	0	ACT+6	ACT	Various	Official
notes, paid	FIN-20-11	LEG2010	CON010	6	3	0	6	MAX3	Various	Official
options contracts	FIN-20-12	FIN3000	ACC100	ACT+6	ACT+3	0	ACT+6	SUP	Finance	Official
options and futures	FIN-20-13	FIN3000	ACC100	ACT+6	ACT+3	0	ACT+6	SUP	Finance	Official
securities sales	FIN-20-14	ACC1000	ACC000	6	3	0	6	MAX1	Accounting	Official
stock investments	FIN-20-15	FIN3000	ACC100	ACT+6	ACT+3	0	ACT+6	SUP	Finance	Official

General

Department / Location Record Series	Record Code	Retention Category	Legal Group	Legal	User	Other	Total	Retention of Copies	Office of Record	Status
client files	GEN-00-01	MIS2000	NONE	0	ACT+1	0	ACT+1	ACT	Various	Official
project files, client	GEN-00-02	MIS2000	NONE	0	ACT+1	0	ACT+1	ACT	Various	Official
reference files	GEN-00-03	REF0000	NONE	0	SUP	0	SUP	SUP	Various	Official

Department / Location Record Series	Record Code	Retention Category	Legal Group	Retention of Official Records				Retention of Copies	Office of Record	Status
				Legal	User	Other	Total			
Legal										
Contract Administration										
buy / sell agreements	LEG-00-02	LEG2000	CON000	ACT+6	ACT+1	0	ACT+6	ACT	Various	Official
contracts, general										
contract compliance	LEG-00-03-01	LEG2010	CON010	6	3	0	6	MAX3	Various	Official
contract working files	LEG-00-03-02	LEG2000	CON000	ACT+6	ACT+1	0	ACT+6	ACT	Various	Official
contracts, changes to	LEG-00-03-03	LEG2000	CON000	ACT+6	ACT+1	0	ACT+6	ACT	Various	Official
employment contracts	LEG-00-03-04	LEG2000	CON000	ACT+6	ACT+1	0	ACT+6	ACT	Various	Official
contracts, government										
accounting records	LEG-00-04-01	LEG2010	CON010	6	3	0	6	MAX3	Various	Official
contract documentation	LEG-00-04-02	LEG2000	CON000	ACT+6	ACT+1	0	ACT+6	ACT	Various	Official
cost accounting	LEG-00-04-03	LEG2010	CON010	6	3	0	6	MAX3	Various	Official
pay administration	LEG-00-04-04	LEG2010	CON010	6	3	0	6	MAX3	Various	Official
procurement	LEG-00-04-05	LEG2010	CON010	6	3	0	6	MAX3	Various	Official
production	LEG-00-04-06	LEG2010	CON010	6	3	0	6	MAX3	Various	Official
salary administration	LEG-00-04-07	LEG2010	CON010	6	3	0	6	MAX3	Various	Official
work products	LEG-00-04-08	LEG2010	CON010	6	3	0	6	MAX3	Various	Official
contracts, improvements to real property										
contract compliance	LEG-00-05-01	LEG2110	CON310	12	3	0	12	MAX3	Various	Official
contract documentation	LEG-00-05-02	LEG2100	CON300	ACT+12	ACT+1	0	ACT+12	ACT	Various	Official
contracts, sales										
contract compliance	LEG-00-06-01	LEG2010	CON010	6	3	0	6	MAX3	Various	Official
contract documentation	LEG-00-06-02	LEG2000	CON000	ACT+6	ACT+1	0	ACT+6	ACT	Various	Official
easements	LEG-00-07	LEG2000	CON000	ACT+6	ACT+1	0	ACT+6	ACT	Various	Official
leases	LEG-00-08	LEG2000	CON000	ACT+6	ACT+1	0	ACT+6	ACT	Various	Official
mortgages	LEG-00-09	LEG2000	CON000	ACT+6	ACT+1	0	ACT+6	ACT	Various	Official
patent agreements	LEG-00-10	LEG2000	CON000	ACT+6	ACT+1	0	ACT+6	ACT	Various	Official
promissory notes	LEG-00-11	LEG2000	CON000	ACT+6	ACT+1	0	ACT+6	ACT	Various	Official
title documentation	LEG-00-12	LEG2000	CON000	ACT+6	ACT+1	0	ACT+6	ACT	Various	Official
warranties, product	LEG-00-13	LEG2000	CON000	ACT+6	ACT+1	0	ACT+6	ACT	Various	Official

XYZ Company
Records Listing With Retention Periods

Department / Location Record Series	Record Code	Retention Category	Legal Group	Retention of Official Records				Retention of Copies	Office of Record	Status
				Legal	User	Other	Total			
Legal (continued)										
General										
legal opinions	LEG-10-01	LEG6010	POL000	ACT+10	IND	0	IND	ACT	Legal	Official
patent applications	LEG-10-02	LEG7000	LIT000	ACT+6	ACT+1	0	ACT+6	ACT	Legal	Official
patents	LEG-10-03	LEG7000	LIT000	ACT+6	ACT+1	0	ACT+6	ACT	Legal	Official
trademark records	LEG-10-04	LEG7000	LIT000	ACT+6	ACT+1	0	ACT+6	ACT	Legal	Official
Legal Compliance										
employment tax filings	LEG-20-01	LEG5010	LEG000	6	10	0	10	MAX3	Legal	Official
excise tax filings	LEG-20-02	LEG5010	LEG000	6	10	0	10	MAX3	Legal	Official
income tax filings	LEG-20-03	LEG5010	LEG000	6	10	0	10	MAX3	Legal	Official
sales tax filings	LEG-20-04	LEG5010	LEG000	6	10	0	10	MAX3	Legal	Official
tax returns	LEG-20-05	LEG5010	LEG000	6	10	0	10	MAX3	Legal	Official
tax returns, employment	LEG-20-06	LEG5010	LEG000	6	10	0	10	MAX3	Legal	Official
tax returns, excise	LEG-20-07	LEG5010	LEG000	6	10	0	10	MAX3	Legal	Official
tax returns, income	LEG-20-08	LEG5010	LEG000	6	10	0	10	MAX3	Legal	Official
tax returns, motor fuel	LEG-20-09	LEG5010	LEG000	6	10	0	10	MAX3	Legal	Official
tax returns, property	LEG-20-10	LEG5010	LEG000	6	10	0	10	MAX3	Legal	Official
tax returns, sales	LEG-20-11	LEG5010	LEG000	6	10	0	10	MAX3	Legal	Official
tax returns, unemployment	LEG-20-12	LEG5010	LEG000	6	10	0	10	MAX3	Legal	Official
tax returns, use	LEG-20-13	LEG5010	LEG000	6	10	0	10	MAX3	Legal	Official
Litigation / Claims										
affidavits	LEG-30-01	LEG4000	LIT000	ACT+6	ACT+1	0	ACT+6	ACT	Legal	Official
claims, affirmative action	LEG-30-02	LEG4000	LIT000	ACT+6	ACT+1	0	ACT+6	ACT	Legal	Official
complaints	LEG-30-03	LEG4000	LIT000	ACT+6	ACT+1	0	ACT+6	ACT	Legal	Official
court case files	LEG-30-04	LEG4000	LIT000	ACT+6	ACT+1	0	ACT+6	ACT	Legal	Official
court records	LEG-30-05	LEG4000	LIT000	ACT+6	ACT+1	0	ACT+6	ACT	Legal	Official
depositions	LEG-30-06	LEG4000	LIT000	ACT+6	ACT+1	0	ACT+6	ACT	Legal	Official
disputes	LEG-30-07	LEG4000	LIT000	ACT+6	ACT+1	0	ACT+6	ACT	Legal	Official

Legal
Litigation / Claims

Department / Location Record Series	Record Code	Retention Category	Legal Group	Retention of Official Records Legal	User Other	Total	Retention of Copies	Office of Record	Status
Legal (continued)									
Litigation / Claims (continued)									
exhibits	LEG-30-08	LEG4000	LIT000	ACT+6	ACT+1	0	ACT+6	ACT	Legal	Official
grievances	LEG-30-09	LEG4000	LIT000	ACT+6	ACT+1	0	ACT+6	ACT	Legal	Official
litigation files	LEG-30-10	LEG4000	LIT000	ACT+6	ACT+1	0	ACT+6	ACT	Legal	Official
Personnel									
Benefits									
actuarial records	PER-00-01	HUM1010	EMP110	ACT+6	ACT+1	0	ACT+6	ACT	Benefits	Official
disability records	PER-00-02	HUM1020	EMP100	6	3	0	6	MAX1	Benefits	Official
education assistance files	PER-00-03	HUM1020	EMP100	6	3	0	6	MAX1	Benefits	Official
employee benefits paid	PER-00-04	HUM1020	EMP100	6	3	0	6	MAX1	Benefits	Official
employee relocation records	PER-00-05	HUM1020	EMP100	6	3	0	6	MAX1	Benefits	Official
employee stock purchase agreements	PER-00-06	HUM1010	EMP110	ACT+6	ACT+1	0	ACT+6	ACT	Benefits	Official
incentive plans	PER-00-07	HUM1010	EMP110	ACT+6	ACT+1	0	ACT+6	ACT	Benefits	Official
pension plan vesting files	PER-00-08	HUM1040	EMP120	6	ACT	0	ACT+6	MAX1	Benefits	Official
pension plans	PER-00-09	HUM1010	EMP110	ACT+6	ACT+1	0	ACT+6	ACT	Benefits	Official
profit sharing plans	PER-00-10	HUM1010	EMP110	ACT+6	ACT+1	0	ACT+6	ACT	Benefits	Official
retirement benefits	PER-00-11	HUM1040	EMP120	6	ACT	0	ACT+6	MAX1	Benefits	Official
retirement plans	PER-00-12	HUM1010	EMP110	ACT+6	ACT+1	0	ACT+6	ACT	Benefits	Official
service records	PER-00-13	HUM3000	EMP300	3	ACT+3	0	ACT+3	SUP	Personnel	Official
sick leave benefits accrued	PER-00-14	HUM1020	EMP100	6	3	0	6	MAX1	Benefits	Official
thrift plan reports	PER-00-15	HUM9900	EMP000	3	3	0	3	MAX1	Various	Official
years of services	PER-00-16	HUM3000	EMP300	3	ACT+3	0	ACT+3	SUP	Personnel	Official
Equal Employment Opportunity									
affirmative action plan	PER-10-01	LEG5000	LEG000	6	6	0	6	MAX1	Legal	Official
form EEO-1	PER-10-02	LEG5000	LEG000	6	6	0	6	MAX1	Legal	Official
form EEO-2	PER-10-03	LEG5000	LEG000	6	6	0	6	MAX1	Legal	Official
racial/ethnic identification (Form EEO-1)	PER-10-04	LEG5000	LEG000	6	6	0	6	MAX1	Legal	Official

XYZ Company
Records Listing With Retention Periods

Personnel (continued)

General

Department/Location Record Series	Record Code	Retention Category	Legal Group	Retention of Official Records				Retention of Copies	Office of Record	Status
				Legal	User	Other	Total			
attendance records	PER-20-01	HUM3010	EMP300	3	3	0	3	MAX1	Personnel	Official
collective bargaining agreements	PER-20-02	LEG2000	CON000	ACT+6	ACT+1	0	ACT+6	ACT	Various	Official
driving exams	PER-20-03	HUM5010	EMP000	3	ACT	0	ACT+3	ACT	Training	Official
employee manuals	PER-20-04	ADM3000	POL000	ACT+10	ACT	0	ACT+10	SUP	Various	Official
job descriptions	PER-20-05	ADM3000	POL000	ACT+10	ACT	0	ACT+10	SUP	Various	Official
labor distribution records	PER-20-06	HUM9900	EMP000	3	3	0	3	MAX1	Various	Official
labor union contracts	PER-20-07	LEG2000	CON000	ACT+6	ACT+1	0	ACT+6	ACT	Various	Official
labor union meetings	PER-20-08	HUM9900	EMP000	3	3	0	3	MAX1	Various	Official
time sheets	PER-20-09	HUM6000	EMP300	3	3	0	3	MAX1	Personnel	Official

Health and Safety

Department/Location Record Series	Record Code	Retention Category	Legal Group	Retention of Official Records				Retention of Copies	Office of Record	Status
				Legal	User	Other	Total			
accident reports	PER-30-01	HUM4020	EMP700	CY+5	3	0	CY+5	MAX1	Safety	Official
damage reports	PER-30-03	HUM4020	EMP700	CY+5	3	0	CY+5	MAX1	Safety	Official
elevator certification	PER-30-04	LEG5020	LEG100	ACT+3	ACT	0	ACT+3	ACT	Legal	Official
emergency action plans	PER-30-05	ADM3000	POL000	ACT+10	ACT	0	ACT+10	SUP	Various	Official
employee exposure records	PER-30-06	HUM4030	EMP500	ACT+30	ACT	0	ACT+30	MAX1	Safety	Official
employee medical complaints	PER-30-07	HUM4010	EMP700	CY+5	3	0	CY+5	MAX1	Safety	Official
employee medical records	PER-30-08	HUM4010	EMP700	CY+5	3	0	CY+5	MAX1	Safety	Official
environmental monitoring records	PER-30-09	ENV1000	ENV200	3	5	0	5	1	Testing	Official
environmental testing methodology	PER-30-10	ENV1000	ENV200	3	5	0	5	1	Testing	Official
environmental testing reports	PER-30-11	ENV1000	ENV200	3	5	0	5	1	Testing	Official
environmental testing worksheets	PER-30-12	ENV1000	ENV200	3	5	0	5	1	Testing	Official
fire extinguisher records	PER-30-13	ADM4000	NONE	0	3	0	3	MAX1	Security	Official
fire prevention programs	PER-30-14	ADM3000	POL000	ACT+10	ACT	0	ACT+10	SUP	Various	Official
hazard communications records	PER-30-15	HUM4031	ENV100	IND	3	0	IND	ACT	Safety	Official
hazardous exposure records	PER-30-16	HUM4030	EMP500	ACT+30	ACT	0	ACT+30	MAX1	Safety	Official
hazardous substance identity records	PER-30-17	HUM4031	ENV100	IND	3	0	IND	ACT	Safety	Official
health and safety bulletins	PER-30-18	HUM4020	EMP700	CY+5	3	0	CY+5	MAX1	Safety	Official
health insurance claims	PER-30-19	HUM1020	EMP100	6	3	0	6	MAX1	Benefits	Official

Department / Location Record Series	Record Code	Retention Category	Legal Group	Retention of Official Records Legal	User	Other	Total	Retention of Copies	Office of Record	Status
Personnel (continued)										
Health and Safety (continued)										
injury reports	PER-30-20	HUM4020	EMP700	CY+5	3	0	CY+5	MAX1	Safety	Official
log, accident (OSHA Form 200)	PER-30-21	HUM4020	EMP700	CY+5	3	0	CY+5	MAX1	Safety	Official
log, injury (OSHA Form 200)	PER-30-22	HUM4020	EMP700	CY+5	3	0	CY+5	MAX1	Safety	Official
material safety data sheets	PER-30-23	HUM4031	ENV100	IND	3	0	IND	ACT	Safety	Official
medical records	PER-30-24	HUM4010	EMP700	CY+5	3	0	CY+5	MAX1	Safety	Official
medical surveillance	PER-30-25	HUM4031	ENV100	IND	3	0	IND	ACT	Safety	Official
noise exposure measurements	PER-30-26	HUM4032	EMP510	2	1	0	2	MAX1	Safety	Official
radiation exposure records	PER-30-27	HUM4030	EMP500	ACT+30	ACT	0	ACT+30	MAX1	Safety	Official
safety inspections	PER-30-28	ADM3010	NONE	0	2	0	2	MAX1	Auditing	Official
safety records	PER-30-29	HUM4020	EMP700	CY+5	3	0	CY+5	MAX1	Safety	Official
supplementary records (OSHA Form 101)	PER-30-30	HUM4020	EMP700	CY+5	3	0	CY+5	MAX1	Safety	Official
toxic substance exposure records	PER-30-31	HUM4030	EMP500	ACT+30	ACT	0	ACT+30	MAX1	Safety	Official
Personnel Actions										
applications, hired	PER-40-01	HUM3010	EMP300	3	3	0	3	MAX1	Personnel	Official
applications, rejected	PER-40-02	HUM2000	EMP900	1	3	0	3	MAX1	Personnel	Official
apprenticeship records	PER-40-03	HUM2000	EMP900	1	3	0	3	MAX1	Personnel	Official
demotion records	PER-40-05	HUM3010	EMP300	3	3	0	3	MAX1	Personnel	Official
education records	PER-40-06	HUM3010	EMP300	3	3	0	3	MAX1	Personnel	Official
employee evaluations	PER-40-07	HUM3010	EMP300	3	3	0	3	MAX1	Personnel	Official
employment actions	PER-40-08	HUM3010	EMP300	3	3	0	3	MAX1	Personnel	Official
employment history, current	PER-40-09	HUM3000	EMP300	3	ACT+3	0	ACT+3	SUP	Personnel	Official
employment history, previous	PER-40-10	HUM3010	EMP300	3	3	0	3	MAX1	Personnel	Official
hiring records	PER-40-11	HUM2000	EMP900	1	3	0	3	MAX1	Personnel	Official
job announcements	PER-40-12	HUM2000	EMP900	1	3	0	3	MAX1	Personnel	Official
layoff records	PER-40-13	HUM3010	EMP300	3	3	0	3	MAX1	Personnel	Official
performance standards	PER-40-14	ADM3000	POL000	ACT+10	ACT	0	ACT+10	SUP	Various	Official
personnel actions	PER-40-15	HUM3010	EMP300	3	3	0	3	MAX1	Personnel	Official
personnel files, active	PER-40-16	HUM3000	EMP300	3	ACT+3	0	ACT+3	SUP	Personnel	Official

XYZ Company
Records Listing With Retention Periods

Department / Location Record Series	Record Code	Retention Category	Legal Group	Retention of Official Records			Retention of Copies	Office of Record	Status
				Legal	User Other	Total			
Personnel (continued)									
Personnel Actions (continued)									
personnel files, terminated	PER-40-17	HUM3010	EMP300	3	3	0	3	MAX1	Personnel	Official
promotion records	PER-40-18	HUM3010	EMP300	3	3	0	3	MAX1	Personnel	Official
tenure records	PER-40-19	HUM3000	EMP300	3	ACT+3	0	ACT+3	SUP	Personnel	Official
termination records	PER-40-20	HUM3010	EMP300	3	3	0	3	MAX1	Personnel	Official
testing records	PER-40-21	HUM2000	EMP900	1	3	0	3	MAX1	Personnel	Official
training records	PER-40-22	HUM5000	EMP000	3	ACT	0	ACT+3	ACT	Training	Official
transfer records	PER-40-23	HUM3010	EMP300	3	3	0	3	MAX1	Personnel	Official
work appraisals	PER-40-24	HUM3010	EMP300	3	3	0	3	MAX1	Personnel	Official
Salary Administration									
bonuses	PER-50-01	HUM6000	EMP300	3	3	0	3	MAX1	Personnel	Official
cost of living records	PER-50-02	HUM6000	EMP300	3	3	0	3	MAX1	Personnel	Official
earnings records	PER-50-03	HUM6000	EMP300	3	3	0	3	MAX1	Personnel	Official
form W-2	PER-50-04	LEG5000	LEG000	6	6	0	6	MAX1	Legal	Official
form W-4	PER-50-05	LEG5000	LEG000	6	6	0	6	MAX1	Legal	Official
pay rates	PER-50-06	HUM6000	EMP300	3	3	0	3	MAX1	Personnel	Official
payroll deductions	PER-50-07	HUM6000	EMP300	3	3	0	3	MAX1	Personnel	Official
salary surveys	PER-50-08	HUM6000	EMP300	3	3	0	3	MAX1	Personnel	Official
time cards	PER-50-09	HUM6000	EMP300	3	3	0	3	MAX1	Personnel	Official
wage rate tables	PER-50-10	HUM6000	EMP300	3	3	0	3	MAX1	Personnel	Official
Product Development									
blueprints	PRD-00-01	MAN1000	MAN000	IND	ACT+5	0	IND	ACT	Operations	Official
design records	PRD-00-02	MAN1000	MAN000	IND	ACT+5	0	IND	ACT	Operations	Official
engineering records	PRD-00-03	MAN1000	MAN000	IND	ACT+5	0	IND	ACT	Operations	Official
laboratory reports	PRD-00-04	MAN2000	MAN000	IND	ACT+5	0	IND	ACT	Operations	Official
product design specifications	PRD-00-05	MAN1000	MAN000	IND	ACT+5	0	IND	ACT	Operations	Official
product testing	PRD-00-06	MAN3000	POL000	ACT+10	ACT+5	0	ACT+10	ACT	Operations	Official

Department / Location Record Series	Record Code	Retention Category	Legal Group	Retention of Official Records				Retention of Copies	Office of Record	Status
				Legal	User	Other	Total			
Product Development (continued)										
production tool design records	PRD-00-07	MAN3000	POL000	ACT+10	ACT+5	0	ACT+10	ACT	Operations	Official
research records	PRD-00-08	MAN1000	MAN000	IND	ACT+5	0	IND	ACT	Operations	Official
testing reports	PRD-00-09	MAN3000	POL000	ACT+10	ACT+5	0	ACT+10	ACT	Operations	Official
Production										
inspection records	PRO-00-01	MAN2000	MAN000	IND	ACT+5	0	IND	ACT	Operations	Official
product inventory	PRO-00-02	ACC2000	ACC100	ACT+6	ACT	0	ACT+6	SUP	Accounting	Official
production costs	PRO-00-03	ACC1000	ACC000	6	3	0	6	MAX1	Accounting	Official
production reports	PRO-00-04	MAN9900	NONE	0	MAX3	0	MAX3	MAX1	Operations	Official
production specifications	PRO-00-05	LEG2010	CON010	6	3	0	6	MAX3	Various	Official
quality control reports	PRO-00-06	MAN2000	MAN000	IND	ACT+5	0	IND	ACT	Operations	Official
warehouse inventory records	PRO-00-07	ACC2000	ACC100	ACT+6	ACT	0	ACT+6	SUP	Accounting	Official
work orders	PRO-00-08	LEG2010	CON010	6	3	0	6	MAX3	Various	Official
work status reports	PRO-00-09	MAN9900	NONE	0	MAX3	0	MAX3	MAX1	Operations	Official
Public Relations										
advertising	PUB-00-01	SAL1000	ADV000	ACT+2	3	0	ACT+3	MAX1	Sales	Official
artwork	PUB-00-02	PUB3000	NONE	0	5	0	5	MAX1	Sales	Official
customer complaints	PUB-00-03	LEG4000	LIT000	ACT+6	ACT+1	0	ACT+6	ACT	Legal	Official
government docket files	PUB-00-04	PUB2000	NONE	0	5	0	5	MAX1	Legal	Official
legislation, pending	PUB-00-05	PUB2000	NONE	0	5	0	5	MAX1	Legal	Official
mailing lists	PUB-00-06	MIS1010	NONE	0	SUP	0	SUP	MAX3	Various	Official
market research data	PUB-00-07	FIN2000	NONE	0	ACT+1	0	ACT+1	ACT	Finance	Official
media packets	PUB-00-08	PUB3000	NONE	0	5	0	5	MAX1	Sales	Official
news releases	PUB-00-09	PUB3000	NONE	0	5	0	5	MAX1	Sales	Official
newsletters, internal	PUB-00-10	PUB4000	NONE	0	3	0	3	MAX1	Personnel	Official
newspaper clippings	PUB-00-11	PUB3000	NONE	0	5	0	5	MAX1	Sales	Official
publicity photographs	PUB-00-12	PUB3000	NONE	0	5	0	5	MAX1	Sales	Official

Department / Location Record Series	Record Code	Retention Category	Legal Group	Retention of Official Records			Retention of Copies	Office of Record	Status
				Legal	User Other	Total			
Public Relations (continued)									
publicity records	PUB-00-13	PUB3000	NONE	0	5	0	5	MAX1	Sales	Official
slide presentations	PUB-00-14	PUB3000	NONE	0	5	0	5	MAX1	Sales	Official
speeches	PUB-00-15	PUB3000	NONE	0	5	0	5	MAX1	Sales	Official
Purchasing									
bids, accepted	PUR-00-01	LEG2000	CON000	ACT+6	ACT+1	0	ACT+6	ACT	Various	Official
bids, rejected	PUR-00-02	FIN8000	NONE	0	3	0	3	MAX1	Finance	Official
catalogs	PUR-00-03	REF0000	NONE	0	SUP	0	SUP	SUP	Various	Official
price lists	PUR-00-04	REF0000	NONE	0	SUP	0	SUP	SUP	Various	Official
purchase orders	PUR-00-05	LEG2000	CON000	ACT+6	ACT+1	0	ACT+6	ACT	Various	Official
quotations	PUR-00-06	FIN8000	NONE	0	3	0	3	MAX1	Finance	Official
receiving documents	PUR-00-07	MIS1000	NONE	0	1	0	1	MAX1	Various	Official
vendor literature	PUR-00-08	REF0000	NONE	0	SUP	0	SUP	SUP	Various	Official
Sales									
back order records	SAL-00-01	MIS1000	NONE	0	1	0	1	MAX1	Various	Official
customer credit files	SAL-00-02	SAL1000	ADV000	ACT+2	3	0	ACT+3	MAX1	Sales	Official
customer lists	SAL-00-03	MIS1010	NONE	0	SUP	0	SUP	MAX3	Various	Official
market surveys	SAL-00-04	ADM1020	NONE	0	ACT+1	0	ACT+1	ACT	Various	Official
marketing plans	SAL-00-05	ADM1020	NONE	0	ACT+1	0	ACT+1	ACT	Various	Official
orders	SAL-00-06	LEG2000	CON000	ACT+6	ACT+1	0	ACT+6	ACT	Various	Official
orders, acknowledgment	SAL-00-07	LEG2010	CON010	6	3	0	6	MAX3	Various	Official
price lists	SAL-00-08	SAL1000	ADV000	ACT+2	3	0	ACT+3	MAX1	Sales	Official
price proposals / quotations	SAL-00-09	SAL1000	ADV000	ACT+2	3	0	ACT+3	MAX1	Sales	Official
product price lists	SAL-00-10	SAL1000	ADV000	ACT+2	3	0	ACT+3	MAX1	Sales	Official
proposals	SAL-00-11	SAL1000	ADV000	ACT+2	3	0	ACT+3	MAX1	Sales	Official
sales activity records	SAL-00-12	MIS1000	NONE	0	1	0	1	MAX1	Various	Official
sales projections	SAL-00-13	ADM1020	NONE	0	ACT+1	0	ACT+1	ACT	Various	Official

XYZ Company
Records Listing With Retention Periods

Department / Location Record Series	Record Code	Retention Category	Legal Group	Retention of Official Records Legal	User	Other	Total	Retention of Copies	Office of Record	Status
Sales (continued)										
sales records	SAL-00-14	ADM9900	NONE	0	MAX3	0	MAX3	MAX1	Various	Official
sales reports	SAL-00-15	MIS1000	NONE	0	1	0	1	MAX1	Various	Official
sales slips	SAL-00-16	ACC1000	ACC000	6	3	0	6	MAX1	Accounting	Official
Shipping / Transportation										
bills of lading	SHP-00-01	LEG2010	CON010	6	3	0	6	MAX3	Various	Official
export declarations	SHP-00-02	LEG5000	LEG000	6	6	0	6	MAX1	Legal	Official
freight records	SHP-00-03	LEG2010	CON010	6	3	0	6	MAX3	Various	Official
packing lists	SHP-00-04	ADM9900	NONE	0	MAX3	0	MAX3	MAX1	Various	Official
shipping instructions	SHP-00-05	ADM9900	NONE	0	MAX3	0	MAX3	MAX1	Various	Official
shipping manifests	SHP-00-06	LEG2010	CON010	6	3	0	6	MAX3	Various	Official
shipping tickets	SHP-00-07	LEG2010	CON010	6	3	0	6	MAX3	Various	Official
waybills	SHP-00-08	LEG2010	CON010	6	3	0	6	MAX3	Various	Official

Appendix C Sample Legal Group File

See Chapter 6 for details about the Legal Group File.

This sample Legal Group File is for a small United States company doing business in Texas. This version of the Legal Group File contains detailed analysis of the legal periods—the minimum and maximum legal periods and citations for the legal requirements and legal considerations—plus the selected and the total legal retention periods. You can also prepare a shorter version of the Legal Group File by excluding the minimum and maximum legal periods and citations and presenting only the selected and the total legal retention periods.

Appendix D contains the Legal Research Index used to produce this report. Appendix E explains the abbreviations used in this appendix.

You should customize the Legal Group File to meet the unique needs of your organization.

Legal Group	Subject	Description		Legal Requirements	Legal Considerations	Total
ACC000	Accounting / Tax General	Includes tax assessment or specific tax requirements for accounts payable, accounts receivable, etc.				
		Legal Requirements:	Minimum	TX: TTC 111.0041 — 3		
			Maximum	US: 26 CFR 31.6001-1 — 4		
			Selected	US: 26 CFR 31.6001-1 — 4		
		Legal Considerations:	Minimum	US: 26 USC 6532	LA1	
			Maximum	US: 26 CFR 301.6501(C)-1	ASIND	
			Selected	US: 26 CFR 301.6501(E)-1	6	
		Selected Legal Retention Period				6
ACC100	Accounting / Tax Capital Acquisitions	Includes depreciation, capital gains and losses, and repairs for capital property				
		Legal Requirements:	Minimum	US: 26 CFR 1.167(E)-1 — ACT		
			Maximum	US: 26 CFR 1.167(E)-1 — ACT		
			Selected	US: 26 CFR 1.167(E)-1 — ACT		
		Legal Considerations:	Minimum	US: 26 CFR 301.6501(A)-1	AS3	
			Maximum	US: 26 CFR 301.6501(C)-1	IND	
			Selected	US: 26 CFR 301.6501(A)-1	6	
		Selected Legal Retention Period				ACT+6
ADV000	Advertising Packaging / Labeling	Includes laws related to promotions, introductory offers, product size advantages, etc. See MAN100 for product liability considerations.				
		Legal Requirements:	Minimum	US: 16 CFR 502.101 — 1		
			Maximum	US: 16 CFR 502.101 — 1		
			Selected	US: 16 CFR 502.101 — 1		
		Legal Considerations:	Minimum	TX: 16.003	LA2	
			Maximum	TX: 16.003	LA2	
			Selected	TX: 16.003 / LIABILITY CONCERNS	ACT+2	
		Selected Legal Retention Period				ACT+2

XYZ Company
Legal Group File

Legal Group	Subject	Description	Legal Requirements	Legal Considerations	Total
BUS000	Business Organization General	Includes requirements for articles of incorporation, partnership documentation, etc. Excludes meeting minutes, shareholder information, etc.			IND
		Legal Requirements: Minimum TX: TCA 2.44	MAINT	
		Maximum TX: TCA 2.44	MAINT	
		Selected TX: TCA 2.44	3	
		Legal Considerations: Minimum TX: TCA 2.44		MAINT
		Maximum LIABILITY CONCERNS		MAINT
		Selected		IND
		Selected Legal Retention Period		
BUS010	Business Organization Former Organizations	Includes requirements for articles of incorporation, partnership documentation, etc. Excludes meeting minutes, shareholder information, etc.			10
		Legal Requirements: Minimum TX: TCA 2.44	MAINT	
		Maximum TX: TCA 2.44	MAINT	
		Selected TX: TCA 2.44	3	
		Legal Considerations: Minimum		NONE
		Maximum		NONE
		Selected LIABILITY CONCERNS		10
		Selected Legal Retention Period		
BUS100	Business Organization Corporation Organization Documentation	Includes requirements for articles of incorporation, partnership documentation, etc. Excludes meeting minutes, shareholder information, etc.			IND
		Legal Requirements: Minimum TX: TCA 2.44	MAINT	
		Maximum TX: TCA 2.44	MAINT	
		Selected TX: TCA 2.44	3	
		Legal Considerations: Minimum		NONE
		Maximum		NONE
		Selected LIABILITY CONCERNS		IND
		Selected Legal Retention Period		

Legal Group	Subject	Description	Legal Requirements		Legal Considerations	Total
BUS110	Business Organization Corporation Shareholder Records	Includes stock transactions, shareholder addresses, etc.				
		The total legal retention period was based upon liability concerns for failure to send notices of meetings and dividends to shareholders and for problems arising out of rights granted by ownership agreements, including purchase of stock.				
		Legal Requirements:	**Minimum**	TX: TCA 2.44	MAINT	
			Maximum	TX: TCA 2.44	MAINT	
			Selected	TX: TCA 2.44	3	
		Legal Considerations:	**Minimum**		NONE	
			Maximum		NONE	
			Selected	LIABILITY CONCERNS AND CON000	ACT+10	
		Selected Legal Retention Period				ACT+10
BUS120	Business Organization Corporation Meetings	Includes minutes and notices from board, shareholder, and committee meetings.				
		Legal Requirements:	**Minimum**	TX: TCA 2.44	MAINT	
			Maximum	TX: TCA 2.44	MAINT	
			Selected	TX: TCA 2.44	3	
		Legal Considerations:	**Minimum**	NONE	0	
			Maximum	NONE	0	
			Selected	LIABILITY CONCERNS	10	
		Selected Legal Retention Period				10
BUS130	Business Organization Corporation Financial Statements	Includes annual financial statements submitted to government agencies and shareholders.				
		Legal Requirements:	**Minimum**	US: 26 USC 6501(A)	3	
			Maximum	TX: TCA 2.44	MAINT	
			Selected	TX: TCA 2.44	3	
		Legal Considerations:	**Minimum**	US: 26 USC 6501(A)	AS3	
			Maximum	US: 26 USC 6501(E)	AS6	
			Selected	US: 26 USC 6501(E) / LIABILITY CONCERNS	10	
		Selected Legal Retention Period				10

Legal Group	Subject	Description		Legal Requirements	Legal Considerations	Total
CON000	Contracts General	Includes documentation for general written contracts, including government contracts. Excludes actual workproducts, deliverable products, or accounting.				
		Legal Requirements:	Minimum	US: 48 CFR 4.703	ACT+3	
			Maximum	US: 48 CFR 4.703	ACT+3	
			Selected	US: 48 CFR 4.703	ACT+3	
		Legal Considerations:	Minimum	TX: TCPRC 16.051	LA4	
			Maximum	MAJORITY OF STATES	LA6	
			Selected	MAJORITY OF STATES	ACT+6	
		Selected Legal Retention Period				ACT+6
CON010	Contracts General Compliance / Work Products	Includes proof of compliance or work products provided under written contracts, including government contracts. Excludes contract documentation.				
		Legal Requirements:	Minimum	US: 48 CFR 4.703	3	
			Maximum	US: 48 CFR 4.705	4	
			Selected	US: 48 CFR 4.705	4	
		Legal Considerations:	Minimum	TX: TCPRC 16.051	LA4	
			Maximum	MAJORITY OF STATES	LA6	
			Selected	MAJORITY OF STATES	6	
		Selected Legal Retention Period				6
CON200	Contracts Liability Insurance	Includes policies and description of coverage for insurance covering liability that may manifest in future years such as hazardous exposure.				
		Legal Requirements:	Minimum		NONE	
			Maximum		NONE	
			Selected	NONE	0	
		Legal Considerations:	Minimum		NONE	
			Maximum		NONE	
			Selected	FUTURE LIABILITY CONCERNS FROM LIT000	IND	
		Selected Legal Retention Period				IND

Legal Group	Subject	Description		Legal Requirements	Legal Considerations	Total
CON300	Contracts Improvements, Real Property	Includes documentation for written contracts related to improvements to real property. excludes actual workproducts, deliverable products, or accounting. Note: liability for injury from improvements to real property may continue indefinitely in some states.	**Legal Requirements:** Minimum Maximum Selected — NONE	NONE NONE 0		
			Legal Considerations: Minimum — TX: TCPRC 16.009 Maximum — TX: TCPRC 16.009 Selected — TX: TCPRC 16.009		LA10 LA12 ACT+12	
			Selected Legal Retention Period			ACT+12
CON310	Contracts Improvements, Real Property Compliance / Work Products	Includes proof of compliance or work products provided under written contracts for improvements to real property. excludes contract documentation.	**Legal Requirements:** Minimum Maximum Selected — NONE	NONE NONE 0		
			Legal Considerations: Minimum — TX: TCPRC 16.051 Maximum — TX: TCPRC 16.051 Selected — TX: TCPRC 16.051		LA10 LA12 12	
			Selected Legal Retention Period			12
EMP000	Employment General	Includes wage rates, job descriptions, work schedules, employment practices and other employment requirements not included elsewhere.	**Legal Requirements:** Minimum — US: 29 CFR 516.6 Maximum — US: 29 CFR 516.5 Selected — US: 29 CFR 516.5	2 3 3		
			Legal Considerations: Minimum Maximum Selected — NONE		NONE NONE 0	
			Selected Legal Retention Period			3

XYZ Company
Legal Group File

Records Retention Program

Legal Group	Subject	Description		Legal Requirements	Legal Considerations	Total
EMP100	Employment Benefits / Pensions Reporting / Contributions	Includes requirements for contributions to and reporting for pension and benefit plans.				
		Legal Requirements:	Minimum	US: 29 CFR 486.5	5	
			Maximum	US: 29 CFR 2610.11	6	
			Selected	US: 29 CFR 2610.11	6	
		Legal Considerations:	Minimum	US: 29 USC 1113	LA3	
			Maximum	US: 29 USC 1113	LA6	
			Selected	US: 29 USC 1113	6	
		Selected Legal Retention Period				6
EMP110	Employment Benefits / Pensions Plans	Includes the actual pension and benefit plans in force.				
		Legal Requirements:	Minimum	US: 29 CFR 2610.11	6	
			Maximum	US: 29 CFR 1627.3	ACT+1	
			Selected	US: 29 CFR 1627.3	ACT+6	
		Legal Considerations:	Minimum	US: 29 USC 1113	LA3	
			Maximum	US: 29 USC 1113	LA6	
			Selected	US: 29 USC 1113	6	
		Selected Legal Retention Period				ACT+6
EMP120	Employment Benefits / Pensions Summary Data	Includes summary of contributions, years of service, benefit accrued, and other information need to implement the benefit and pension plans.				
		Legal Requirements:	Minimum	US: 29 CFR 2610.11	6	
			Maximum	US: 29 CFR 2610.11	6	
			Selected	US: 29 CFR 2610.11	6	
		Legal Considerations:	Minimum	US: 29 CFR 1113	LA3	
			Maximum	US: 29 CFR 1113	LA6	
			Selected	US: 29 USC 1113	6	
		Selected Legal Retention Period				6

Legal Group	Subject	Description		Legal Requirements	Legal Considerations	Total
EMP300	Employment Employment Actions	Includes requirements related to specific employee personnel actions such as hiring, firing, promotion, work schedules, etc.				
		Legal Requirements:	Minimum Maximum Selected	US: 29 CFR 1602.14 US: 20 CFR 655.102 US: 20 CFR 655.102	1 3 3	
		Legal Considerations:	Minimum Maximum Selected	NONE	NONE NONE 0	
		Selected Legal Retention Period				3
EMP500	Employment Health and Safety Hazardous Exposure	Includes requirements related to work-related exposure to hazardous substances.				
		Legal Requirements:	Minimum Maximum Selected	US: 29 CFR 1910.1001 US: 29 CFR 1910.20(d) US: 29 CFR 1910.20	20 ACT+30 ACT+30	
		Legal Considerations:	Minimum Maximum Selected	RISK ASSESSMENT	NONE NONE ACT+30	
		Selected Legal Retention Period				ACT+30
EMP510	Employment Health and Safety Noise Exposure Measurements	Includes requirements related to measurement of noise in work environment.				
		Legal Requirements:	Minimum Maximum Selected	US: 29 CFR 1910.95 US: 29 CFR 1910.95 US: 29 CFR 1910.95	2 2 2	
		Legal Considerations:	Minimum Maximum Selected	NONE	NONE NONE 0	
		Selected Legal Retention Period				2

Legal Group	Subject	Description		Legal Requirements	Legal Considerations	Total
EMP511	Employment Health and Safety Audiometric Test Record	Includes requirements related to audiometric tests conducted for employees.				
			Legal Requirements: Minimum	US: 29 CFR 1910.95	ACT	
			Maximum	US: 29 CFR 1910.95	ACT	
			Selected	US: 29 CFR 1910.95	ACT	
			Legal Considerations: Minimum	NONE	0	
			Maximum	NONE	0	
			Selected	NONE	0	
			Selected Legal Retention Period			ACT
EMP700	Employment Health and Safety Illness / Accident	Includes requirements related to work-related illness and accident, including workers compensation.				
			Legal Requirements: Minimum	US: 29 CFR 1904.6	CY+5	
			Maximum	US: 29 CFR 1904.6	CY+5	
			Selected	US: 29 CFR 1904.6	CY+5	
			Legal Considerations: Minimum	TX: 8307-4a	LA1	
			Maximum	TX: 8307-7	MAINT	
			Selected	TX: 8307-7	3	
			Selected Legal Retention Period			CY+5
EMP710	Employment Health and Safety Emergency Action Plans	Includes requirements related to fire prevention plans and other emergency action plans.				
			Legal Requirements: Minimum	US: 29 CFR 1910.38	ACT	
			Maximum	US: 29 CFR 1910.38	ACT	
			Selected	US: 29 CFR 1910.38	ACT	
			Legal Considerations: Minimum	NONE	0	
			Maximum	NONE	0	
			Selected	NONE	0	
			Selected Legal Retention Period			ACT

Legal Group	Subject	Description		Legal Requirements	Legal Considerations	Total
EMP711	Employment Health and Safety Fire Protection	Includes requirements related to testing of fire protection equipment.				
		Legal Requirements:	Minimum	US: 29 CFR 1910.157		
				1		
			Maximum	US: 29 CFR 1910.157		
				1		
			Selected	US: 29 CFR 1910.157		
				1		
		Legal Considerations:	Minimum		NONE	
			Maximum		NONE	
			Selected	NONE	0	
		Selected Legal Retention Period				1
EMP900	Employment Selection General	Includes requirements related to advertising, interviewing, testing, selecting, and hiring.				
		Legal Requirements:	Minimum	US: 29 CFR 1627.3		
				1		
			Maximum	US: 29 CFR 1627.3		
				1		
			Selected	US: 29 CFR 1627.3		
				1		
		Legal Considerations:	Minimum		NONE	
			Maximum		NONE	
			Selected	NONE	0	
		Selected Legal Retention Period				1
ENV100	Environment Hazardous Substances General	Includes records related to the manufacture, use, testing and disposal of hazardous substances.				
		Legal Requirements:	Minimum	US: 40 CFR 306.32		
				6		
			Maximum	US: 29 CFR 1910.20		
				30		
			Selected	US: 29 CFR 1910.20		
				30		
		Legal Considerations:	Minimum		NONE	
			Maximum		NONE	
			Selected	RISK ASSESSMENT	IND	
		Selected Legal Retention Period				IND

XYZ Company
Legal Group File

Legal Group	Subject	Description		Legal Requirements	Legal Considerations	Total
ENV110	Environment Hazardous Substances Transportation	Includes records related to the transportation of hazardous substances such as manifests.				
		Legal Requirements:	Minimum	US: 40 CFR 263.20		
			Maximum	US: 40 CFR 263.20		
			Selected	US: 40 CFR 263.20	3	
		Legal Considerations:	Minimum		NONE	
			Maximum		NONE	
			Selected		0	
		Selected Legal Retention Period		NONE		3
ENV200	Environment Water Pollution	Records related to testing and monitoring of water.				
		Legal Requirements:	Minimum	US: 40 CFR 112.7(E)		
			Maximum	US: 40 CFR 144.28I		
			Selected	US: 40 CFR 144.28I	3	
		Legal Considerations:	Minimum		NONE	
			Maximum		NONE	
			Selected		0	
		Selected Legal Retention Period		NONE		3
LEG000	Legal Compliance General	Include records of compliance with state and federal laws not specifically covered elsewhere.				
		Legal Requirements:	Minimum		NONE	
			Maximum		NONE	
			Selected	NONE	0	
		Legal Considerations:	Minimum		NONE	
			Maximum		NONE	
			Selected	RISK ASSESSMENT	6	
		Selected Legal Retention Period				6

XYZ Company
Legal Group File

Records Retention Program

Legal Group	Subject	Description		Legal Requirements	Legal Considerations	Total
LEG100	Legal Compliance Business Licenses / Orders	Includes licenses and permits required to do business and regulatory orders governing the conduct of business.				
			Legal Requirements: Minimum Maximum Selected	NONE NONE 0	NONE NONE	
			Legal Considerations:	TO ENSURE LEGAL COMPLIANCE	ACT+3	
			Selected Legal Retention Period			ACT+3
LIT000	Litigation / Claims General	Includes litigation and claims documentation, including judgments, for use in similar cases.				
			Legal Requirements: Minimum Maximum Selected	NONE NONE 0	NONE	
			Legal Considerations: Minimum Maximum Selected	TX: TCPRC 16.003 US: 28 USC 2401(A) IN CASE OF SIMILAR ACTIONS	LA2 LA6 ACT+6	
			Selected Legal Retention Period			ACT+6
MAN000	Manufacturing Product Liability	Includes records related to the design and manufacture of products for potential use in future product liability suits. from date on first sale				
			Legal Requirements: Minimum Maximum Selected	NONE NONE 0	NONE	
			Legal Considerations: Minimum Maximum Selected	TX: TCPRC 16.003 PRODUCT LIABILITY TX: TCPRC 16.003 / LIABILITY CONCERNS	LA2 IND IND	
			Selected Legal Retention Period			IND

Records Retention Program

XYZ Company
Legal Group File

Legal Group	Subject	Description	Legal Requirements	Legal Considerations	Total
NONE	No legal period	No legal retention requirement identified after adequate legal research.			
		Legal Requirements: Minimum Maximum Selected NONE	NONE NONE 0		
		Legal Considerations: Minimum Maximum Selected NONE		NONE NONE 0	
		Selected Legal Retention Period			0
POL000	Policies / Procedures	Includes policies for areas such as employment, records management, accounting, purchasing, quality control, etc.			
		Legal Requirements: Minimum Maximum Selected NONE	NONE NONE 0		
		Legal Considerations: Minimum Maximum Selected MAXIMUM PERIOD FOR LEGAL LIABILITY		NONE NONE ACT+10	
		Selected Legal Retention Period			ACT+10
POL100	Policies / Procedures Records Retention	Includes program development and documentation of destruction.			
		Legal Requirements: Minimum Maximum Selected NONE	NONE NONE 0		
		Legal Considerations: Minimum Maximum Selected TO SHOW COMPLIANCE WITH PROGRAM		NONE NONE 10	
		Selected Legal Retention Period			10

Appendix D Sample Legal Research Index

See Chapter 4 for details about the Records Retention Schedule. The federal laws appear in *Recordkeeping Requirements* . The Texas laws appear in *Legal Requirements for Business Records: State Requirements*. The full text of these laws can also be found in most law libraries.

This sample Legal Research Index contains information from the legal research for a small United States company doing business in Texas.

Appendix E explains the abbreviations used in this appendix.

You should customize the Legal Research Index to meet the unique needs of your organization.

XYZ Company
Legal Research Index

Jur.	Citation	LRBR Code	Subjects	Legal Group	Legal Period	Records Affected / Agency
TX	TCPRC 16.004	TX 115-0020-00	limitation of actions account, open	ACC000	LA4	
TX	TRCSA 5221b-9	TX 130-0040-00	employment unemployment compensation	ACC000	MAINT	
TX	TTC 111.0041	TX 150-0005-00	tax general	ACC000	4	
TX	TTC 111.201	TX 150-0010-00	tax general	ACC000	AS4	
TX	TTC 111.203	TX 150-0020-00	tax general	ACC000	LAIND	extensions
TX	TTC 151.025	TX 150-0030-00	tax sales	ACC000	4	
TX	TTC 151.026	TX 150-0040-00	tax sales	ACC000	MAINT	
TX	TTC 152.063	TX 150-0050-00	tax sales	ACC000	4	
TX	TTC 152.103	TX 150-0060-00	tax sales	ACC000	4	
TX	TTC 154.208	TX 150-0160-00	tax sales	ACC000	2	
TX	TTC 157.203	TX 150-0280-00	tax transportation	ACC000	3	
TX	TTC 191.085	TX 150-0290-00	tax occupation	ACC000	2	
TX	Rule 3.281	TX 210-0010-00	tax sales	ACC000	MAINT	Comptroller to Public Accounts
TX	Rule 3.286	TX 210-0020-00	tax sales	ACC000	4	Comptroller to Public Accounts
TX	40 TAC 301.6	TX 230-0010-00	employment unemployment compensation	ACC000	4	Texas Employment Commission

XYZ Company
Legal Research Index

Jur.	Citation	LRBR Code	Subjects	Legal Group	Legal Period	Records Affected / Agency
US	26 USC 6501(A)	US 126-0060-00	tax general - assessment	ACC000	AS3	accounting records Internal Revenue Service
US	26 USC 6501(C)	US 126-0070-00	tax general - assessment fraud	ACC000	ASIND	accounting records Internal Revenue Service
US	26 USC 6501(E)	US 126-0070-00	tax general - assessment understatements by 25%	ACC000	AS6	accounting records Internal Revenue Service
US	26 USC 6502	US 126-0110-00	tax general - collection	ACC000	LA6	accounting records Internal Revenue Service
US	26 USC 6511(A)	US 126-0120-00	tax general - credit/refund	ACC000	LA2	accounting records Internal Revenue Service
US	26 USC 6511(D)	US 126-0120-00	tax general - credit/refund bad debt	ACC000	LA7	accounting records Internal Revenue Service
US	26 USC 6532	US 126-0150-00	tax general - taxpayer suit	ACC000	LA2	accounting records Internal Revenue Service
US	26 USC 6532	US 126-0150-00	tax general - taxpayer suit	ACC000	LA1	accounting records Internal Revenue Service
US	26 USC 7203	US 126-0180-00	tax general - assessment failure to file	ACC000	ASIND	accounting records Internal Revenue Service
US	26 USC 7203	US 126-0180-00	tax general - assessment failure to file	ACC000	ASIND	accounting records Internal Revenue Service
US	29 USC 255	US 129-0020-00	employment wage, recovery of	ACC000	LA2	payroll records Labor, Department of
US	26 CFR 1.666(D)-1A(A)	US 226-0630-00	tax income - trusts	ACC000	ACT	accounting records Internal Revenue Service
US	26 CFR 1.6001-1	US 226-0970-00	tax income	ACC000	IND	accounting records Internal Revenue Service
US	26 CFR 31.6001-1	US 226-1090-00	tax employment	ACC000	4	payroll records Internal Revenue Service

XYZ Company
Legal Research Index

Jur.	Citation	LRBR Code	Subjects	Legal Group	Legal Period	Records Affected / Agency
US	26 CFR 31.6001-2	US 226-1100-00	tax employment	ACC000	4	payroll records Internal Revenue Service
US	26 CFR 31.6001-4	US 226-1130-00	tax employment	ACC000	4	payroll records;unemployment taxes Internal Revenue Service
US	26 CFR 31.6001-5	US 226-1150-00	tax employment	ACC000	4	payroll records Internal Revenue Service
US	26 CFR 301.6501(A)-1	US 226-1870-00	tax income - assessment general	ACC000	AS3	accounting records Internal Revenue Service
US	26 CFR 301.6501(C)-1	US 226-1880-00	tax income - assessment fraud	ACC000	ASIND	accounting records Internal Revenue Service
US	26 CFR 301.6501(E)-1	US 226-1890-00	tax gift - assessment understatement by 25%	ACC000	AS6	accounting records Internal Revenue Service
US	26 CFR 301.6501(E)-1	US 226-1890-00	tax income - assessment understatement by 25%	ACC000	AS6	accounting records Internal Revenue Service
US	26 CFR 301.6532-1(A)	US 226-1960-00	tax income - suit	ACC000	LA2	accounting records Internal Revenue Service
US	26 CFR 301.6532-2	US 226-1970-00	tax income - suit	ACC000	LA2	accounting records Internal Revenue Service
US	29 CFR 5.5	US 229-0040-00	contract federal - payroll	ACC000	3	payroll records Labor, Department of
US	29 CFR 516.5	US 229-0300-00	employment payroll records	ACC000	3	payroll records Labor, Department of: Wage and Hour Division
US	29 CFR 1620.22(B)	US 229-0910-00	limitation of actions wages, recovery of	ACC000	LA3	payroll records Equal Employment Opportunity Commission
US	29 CFR 1627.3(A)	US 229-0920-00	employment payroll	ACC000	3	payroll records Equal Employment Opportunity Commission
US	31 CFR 315.29(C)	US 231-0120-00	bonds United States	ACC000	LA6	bond records Treasury, Department of the

XYZ Company
Legal Research Index

Jur.	Citation	LRBR Code	Subjects	Legal Group	Legal Period	Records Affected / Agency
US	48 CFR 4.705	US 248-0050-00	contract, government compliance procurement	ACC000	4	procurement
US	26 CFR 1.167(E)-1	US 226-0190-00	tax income - depreciation	ACC100	ACT	accounting records Internal Revenue Service
US	26 CFR 301.6501(A)-1	US 226-1870-00	tax income - assessment general	ACC100	AS3	accounting records Internal Revenue Service
US	26 CFR 301.6501(E)-1	US 226-1890-00	tax income - assessment understate by 25%	ACC100	AS6	accounting records Internal Revenue Service
TX	TCPRC 16.003	TX 114-0010-00	limitations of action general	ADV000	LA2	
US	16 USC 502.100	US 116-0150-00	advertising general	ADV000	CY+1	Federal Trade Commission
US	16 USC 502.101	US 116-0155-00	advertising general	ADV000	CY+1	Federal Trade Commission
US	16 USC 502.102	US 116-0160-00	advertising general	ADV000	CY+1	Federal Trade Commission
TX	TCA 2.44	TX 140-0010-00	business organization corporation	BUS000	MAINT	
TX	TCA 2.44	TX 140-0010-00	business organization corporation	BUS010	MAINT	
TX	TCA 2.44	TX 140-0010-00	business organization corporation	BUS100	MAINT	
TX	TCA 2.44	TX 140-0010-00	business organization corporation	BUS110	MAINT	
TX	TCA 2.44	TX 140-0010-00	business organization corporation	BUS120	MAINT	
TX	TCA 2.44	TX 140-0010-00	business organization corporation	BUS130	MAINT	

XYZ Company
Legal Research Index

Jur.	Citation	LRBR Code	Subjects	Legal Group	Legal Period	Records Affected / Agency
US	26 USC 6501 (A)	US 126-0060-00	tax general - assessment	BUS130	AS3	accounting records Internal Revenue Service
US	26 CFR 6501 (E)	US 126-0070-00	tax general - assessment understatements by 25%	BUS130	AS6	accounting records Internal Revenue Service
TX	TBCC-UCC 2.725	TX 110-0010-00	limitation of actions contract, sales	CON000	LA4	
TX	TCPRC 16.051	TX 115-0060-00	limitation of actions contract, written	CON000	LA4	
US	28 USC 2401	US 128-0040-00	limitation of actions injury, personal	CON000	LA3	
US	28 USC 2401	US 128-0040-00	limitation of actions injury, personal	CON000	LA6	
US	48 CFR 4.703	US 248-0034-00	contract federal	CON000	ACT+3	contract records
US	28 USC 2401	US 128-0040-00	limitation of actions injury, personal	CON010	LA6	
US	28 USC 2401	US 128-0040-00	limitation of actions injury, personal	CON010	LA3	
US	48 CFR 4.703	US 248-0034-00	contract, government compliance	CON010	3	contract records
US	48 CFR 4.705	US 248-0050-00	contract, government compliance cost accounting	CON010	4	cost accounting
TX	TCPRC 16.008	TX 115-0040-00	limitation of actions property, real - improvements	CON300	LA10	
TX	TCPRC 16.008	TX 115-0040-00	limitation of actions property, real - improvements	CON300	LA12	
TX	TCPRC 16.009	TX 115-0050-00	limitation of actions property, real - improvements	CON300	LA10	
TX	TCPRC 16.009	TX 115-0050-00	limitation of actions property, real - improvements	CON300	LA12	

XYZ Company
Legal Research Index

Jur.	Citation	LRBR Code	Subjects	Legal Group	Legal Period	Records Affected / Agency
TX	TCPRC 16.008	TX 115-0040-00	limitation of actions property, real - improvements	CON310	LA10	
TX	TCPRC 16.008	TX 115-0040-00	limitation of actions property, real - improvements	CON310	LA12	
TX	TCPRC 16.009	TX 115-0050-00	limitation of actions property, real - improvements	CON310	LA10	
TX	TCPRC 16.009	TX 115-0050-00	limitation of actions property, real - improvements	CON310	LA12	
US	29 CFR 516.5	US 229-0300-00	employment payroll records	EMP000	3	Labor, Department of: Wage and Hour Division
US	29 CFR 516.6	US 229-0310-00	employment earnings and wage rates	EMP000	2	earnings records; wage rate tables Labor, Department of: Wage and Hour Division
US	29 USC 1027	US 129-0050-00	employment pension/retirement	EMP100	6	pension plan reports Labor, Department of
US	29 USC 1113	US 129-0070-00	employment pension/retirement	EMP100	LA3	pension contributions; service Labor, Department of
US	29 USC 1113	US 129-0070-00	employment pension/retirement	EMP100	LA6	pension contributions; service Labor, Department of
US	29 USC 1451	US 129-0080-00	employment pension/retirement	EMP100	LA6	pension contributions; service Labor, Department of
US	29 USC 1451	US 129-0080-00	employment pension/retirement	EMP100	LA3	pension contributions; service Labor, Department of
US	29 CFR 486.5	US 229-0240-00	employment labor relations - pension	EMP100	5	pension records Labor, Department of: Labor-Management Standards Enforcement
US	29 CFR 2610.11	US 229-1590-00	employment benefits contributions	EMP100	6	premium payment Pension Benefit Guaranty Corporation
US	29 USC 1113	US 129-0070-00	employment pension/retirement	EMP110	LA6	pension contributions; service Labor, Department of
US	29 USC 1451	US 129-0080-00	employment pension/retirement	EMP110	LA6	pension contributions; service Labor, Department of

XYZ Company
Legal Research Index

Jur.	Citation	LRBR Code	Subjects	Legal Group	Legal Period	Records Affected / Agency
US	29 CFR 1627.3	US 229-0920-00	employment benefits / pensions plans	EMP110	ACT+1	benefit plan records Equal Employment Opportunity Commission
US	29 USC 1113	US 129-0070-00	employment pension/retirement	EMP120	LA6	pension contributions; service Labor, Department of
US	29 USC 1451	US 129-0080-00	employment pension/retirement	EMP120	LA6	pension contributions; service Labor, Department of
US	29 CFR 2610.11	US 229-1590-00	employment benefits contributions	EMP120	6	premium payment Pension Benefit Guaranty Corporation
US	20 CFR 655.102	US 220-0057-00	employment wage and hour	EMP300	3	labor certificates Labor, Department of
US	29 CFR 1602.14	US 229-0780-00	employment personnel action	EMP300	1	employee files;promotion;termination Equal Employment Opportunity Commission
US	29 CFR 1627.3	US 229-0920-00	employment personnel action	EMP300	1	employee files;promotion;termination Equal Employment Opportunity Commission
US	48 CFR 4.705	US 248-0050-00	contract, government compliance time cards	EMP300	2	time cards
TX	TRCSA 5182b	TX 130-0035-00	employment health and safety	EMP500	30	workplace chemical list
TX	TRCSA 5182b	TX 130-0035-00	employment health and safety	EMP500	MAINT	material safety data sheets
US	29 CFR 1910.20(d)	US 229-1030-00	employment health and safety - medical records	EMP500	ACT+30	employee medical records Occupational Safety and Health Administration
US	29 CFR 1910.20(d)	US 229-1030-00	employment health and safety - hazardous exposure	EMP500	30	employee exposure records;exposure tests Occupational Safety and Health Administration
US	29 CFR 1910.1001	US 229-1180-00	employment health and safety - hazardous substance	EMP500	20	medical records - asbestos exposure Occupational Safety and Health Administration
US	29 CFR 1910.95	US 229-1070-00	employment health and safety noise exposure	EMP510	2	noise exposure measurements Occupational Safety and Health Administration

XYZ Company
Legal Research Index

Jur.	Citation	LRBR Code	Subjects	Legal Group	Legal Period	Records Affected / Agency
US	29 CFR 1910.95	US 229-1070-00	employment / health and safety - noise exposure	EMP511	ACT	noise tests / Occupational Safety and Health Administration
TX	TRCSA 8307-4a	TX 130-0120-00	employment / workers' compensation	EMP700	LA1	
TX	TRCSA 8307-7	TX 130-0130-00	employment / workers' compensation	EMP700	MAINT	
US	29 CFR 1904.6	US 229-1000-00	employment / health and safety - injury/illness	EMP700	CY+5	accident/illness logs and summaries / Occupational Safety and Health Administration
US	29 CFR 1910.38	US 229-1060-00	employment / health and safety / emergency action plan	EMP710	ACT	emergency action plan / Occupational Safety and Health Administration
US	29 CFR 1910.157	US 229-1100-00	employment / health and safety - fire protection	EMP711	1	fire extinguisher tests / Occupational Safety and Health Administration
US	29 CFR 1627.3	US 229-0920-00	employment / employee selection	EMP900	1	applications;ads; hiring decisions / Equal Employment Opportunity Commission
US	40 CFR 264.73	US 240-0780-00	environment / hazardous substance / waste disposal sites	ENV100	ACT	hazardous waste facility records / Environmental Protection Agency
US	40 CFR 306.32	US 240-0965-00	environment / hazardous substance / general	ENV100	6	CERCLA cost documentation / Environmental Protection Agency
US	40 CFR 306.32	US 240-0965-00	environment / hazardous substance / general	ENV100	6	CERCLA cost documentation / Environmental Protection Agency
US	40 CFR 263.20	US 240-0738-00	environment / hazardous substance / transportation	ENV110	3	manifest; transportation log / Environmental Protection Agency
US	40 CFR 112.7(e)	US 240-0450-00	environment / water pollution	ENV200	3	spill prevention plan / Environmental Protection Agency
US	40 CFR 144.28(l)	US 240-0515-00	environment / water pollution / well, underwater injection: class I, II, III	ENV200	3	testing; monitoring; calibration; maintenance / Environmental Protection Agency

XYZ Company
Legal Research Index

Jur.	Citation	LRBR Code	Subjects	Legal Group	Legal Period	Records Affected / Agency
US	40 CFR 144.31(f)	US 240-0520-00	environment water pollution well, underground injection	ENV200	3	permit application data Environmental Protection Agency
US	40 CFR 144.51(l)(2)(i)	US 240-0530-00	environment water pollution well, underground injection	ENV200	3	pollution monitoring: calibration/maintenance Environmental Protection Agency
TX	TCPRC 16.003	TX 115-0010-00	limitation of actions injury, personal	LIT000	LA2	
US	28 USC 2401(A)	US 128-0040-00	limitation of actions other	LIT000	LA6	
US	28 USC 2401(B)	US 128-0040-00	limitation of actions injury, personal	LIT000	LA3	

Appendix E

Abbreviations of Legal and Records Retention Periods

You will use abbreviations frequently to represent legal periods or records retention periods for several reasons:

- Abbreviations are easier to understand and use than long, cumbersome legal phrases.

- Abbreviations need less space in reports and databases.

- Abbreviations can be converted into mathematical statements for determining the longest of several periods.

This appendix reviews the various abbreviations used in this workbook to represent legal periods and records retention periods.

ABBREVIATIONS

Legal Periods

Legal periods represent periods stated in laws that may affect the retention of your records. Common legal periods include specific retention periods, statutes of limitation and limitation of assessment. Laws that require you to keep records but do not state a specific retention period can also be converted to a legal period.

The following abbreviations for legal periods are used in the Legal Research Index and in the Legal Group File for the

See Chapter 4 for information on the types of laws that state legal periods for records retention purposes. See also Chapter 6 for in-depth analysis on how to interpret and apply these legal periods to your records retention program.

minimum and maximum legal requirements and legal considerations periods:

- *ATX*: ACT+TAX. The period of time after the matter is active and after the tax filing date. See also "TAX" below.

- *AS*: limitation of assessment. The period of time the tax agency can determine whether you have paid the correct amount of taxes. "LA" could also be used for "limitation of assessment" when "SL" is used for "statute of limitation." See also "TAX" below.

- *CY*: current year. A period of time starting after the end of the current calendar year—December 31.

- *D*: days.

- *LA*: limitation of action. The period of time a legal action or law suit can be brought. This term is used by many states instead of "statute of limitations" and by other states for time periods for legal actions addressed in regulations.

- *IND*: indefinite. A long period of time that cannot be determined in advance.

- *MAINT*: maintain. A requirement to keep records that does not state a specific retention period. Many interpret this to mean a retention period of no longer than 3 years.

- *M*: months.

- *SL*: statute of limitations. Same as "limitation of actions."

- *TAX*: tax filing date. A legal period starting from the date you filed a tax return or the tax return was due, whichever occurred later.

- *Y*: years. Legal periods will be in "years" unless otherwise specified.

- *number*. A specific period of time for retention specified by the law.

- +: plus. A time period consisting of two or more components.

Normally express time periods in years, unless months or days are used in the law.

Record Retention Periods

Records retention periods reflect the actual periods you will keep records for legal, user, total or other purposes. They represent your assessment of how long users need records to do their jobs and how long your organization needs to keep records to comply with the law or protect itself from legal consequences. You use judgment, experience and expertise to determine these periods.

The following abbreviations of retention periods are used in the Records Retention Schedule, the Records Listing With Records Retention Periods and the Legal Group File for selected and total legal retention periods.

- *ACT*: active. The period while a matter is active.

- *ACY*: ACT+CY. The period of time starting after the matter is no longer active and after the end of the current calendar year.

- *CY*: current year. A period of time starting after the end of the current calendar year—December 31.

- *D*: days.

- *IND*: indefinite. A long period of time that cannot be determined in advance.

- *M*: months.

- *MAX(number)*: maximum. Retain records for no longer than the maximum period stated. They may be destroyed earlier than the period stated if no longer needed. This retention period may only be used for general administrative records, miscellaneous correspondence, and other records possessing little value that can be destroyed within a few years.

- *SUP*: superseded. Retain records until they are replace by more current versions. Similar to ACT, but records cease to be active when they are placed.

- Y: years. Retention periods will be in "years" unless otherwise specified.

- *(number)*. A specific period of time for retention specified by the law.

- +: plus. A time period consisting of two or more components.

Normally express time periods in years, unless months or days are used in the law.

COMPARISONS USING LEGAL AND RECORDS RETENTION PERIODS

You will need to perform comparisons and calculations on legal and records retention periods to complete the following steps of the records retention program.

- *The Legal Group File*: determining the minimum and maximum legal consideration and legal requirement period for each legal group.

- *The Legal Group File*: determining the total legal retention period by calculating the longest retention period between the selected legal requirement period and the selected legal consideration period for each legal group.

- *The Records Retention Schedule*: determining the total retention period based upon the legal, user and any other retention periods.

You can quickly determine the longest numeric retention period by comparing the numerical values. But comparisons generally are not that easy. Many periods use alphabetic abbreviations to generally reflect starting points for retention or events. Other retention periods consist of combinations of alphabetic abbreviations and numerical values.

The following sections provide some of the rules for comparing legal or retention periods. If you use different abbreviations, you should also establish appropriate rules.

Alphabetic Abbreviations

Alphabetic abbreviations either reflect the starting time or event for retention purposes (e.g., ACT—keep the records while they are active) or a special condition relation to retention (e.g., IND—keep the records for an "indefinite" period). Even though they are non-numeric expressions, they must still be compared to determine the longest period among several entries.

The following alphabetic abbreviations are listed in their general order of precedent (longest to shortest retention periods).

- IND (indefinite)

- ACY (active plus current year)

- ACT (active)

- SUP (superseded)

- MAX (maximum)

- CY (current year)

Some alphabetic conditions such as ACT may actually be shorter than CY. The abbreviation ACY (active plus current year) was developed to resolve that conflict. The MAX designation may also be shorter than CY in some circumstances, but could be longer in others.

Alpha-numeric Abbreviations

Frequently, a specific period of time (e.g., 5 years) is modified by an alphabetic abbreviation (e.g., CY). The resulting alpha-numeric expression reflects the combination of the two periods (e.g., CY+5). For consistency, state the alphabetic portion first and then the numeric value. Place a "+" between the part to indicate that the periods are added together. If the periods are not added together (e.g., MAX3), no plus sign is used.

Determining the Longest Period

The longest legal or retention period can generally be determined by following of these rules.

- *Numerical Periods.* Select the longest numerical period. If you stated the numerical period with a period modifier other than years (Y), convert all the periods to the same modifier.

- *Alphabetic Periods.* Select the alphabetic period highest on the precedent list above.

- *Alpha-numeric Periods.* Select the alphabetic periods highest on the precedent list above plus the longest numeric period. The alphabetic and numeric periods can each be selected from different legal or retention periods.

The following exceptions also apply.

In this example, you could alternatively use the ACY+3 abbreviation.

- If the numerical period associated with a "CY" retention period is the longest numerical period, then then total retention period will be the longest numerical period plus one (3+1=4). For example, the total retention period for a legal period of CY+3 and a user period of ACT is ACT+4.

Records Retention Procedures

- If the longest alphabetic period is MAX do not include the "+." The total retention of MAX3 results from a legal period of 3 and a user period of MAX1.

- The longest retention period is IND. Even if one period is IND and the other a numeric period, the total is still IND.

The examples below indicate the total retention periods based upon the legal and user periods:

Legal Period	User Period	Total Period
3	4	4
3	IND	IND
ACT	IND	IND
3	CY+1	3
3	MAX1	3
ACT+3	6	ACT+6
ACT+3	ACT+4	ACT+4
ACT+3	CY+3	ACT+4
ACT+3	CY+3	ACY+3

Appendix F   Risk Assessment

Organizations face critical legal decisions related to their records and information management programs. What records must be maintained to meet the requirements of state and federal agencies? How long must our records be maintained?

Lawyers may provide the answers to these complex legal issues. In some cases they will determine the precise actions to be followed by an organization. In other cases they will suggest possible alternative approaches.

See Chapter 6 for details regarding legal requirements and legal considerations.

In many areas of records and information management affected by the law, the answers are not precise. For example, while some laws clearly specify the minimum period of time records must be maintained, others merely state the requirement to keep records but do not specify the retention period. The clearly stated, specific requirements to keep records may be "legal requirements" while the more nebulous, imprecise areas of law may be "legal considerations." The interaction between records managers, lawyers, and others in our organizations will depend upon whether a legal requirement or legal consideration is involved.

Risk is a Business Decision

One of the major responsibilities of an organization's management is to make difficult decisions regarding organizational activities. Should a particular project be initiated this year, next year, or at all? Should we start manufacturing a new product? Should we continue manufacturing an old one? Should we expand our operation through acquisition or sell off on profitable divisions? All these decisions, and many more regularly made by business managers, require an assessment of the pros and cons of one approach versus another or the risks of action versus the risks of inaction.

These business managers have attained high positions within an organization because of their experience and ability to make these difficult decisions. When the welfare of the organization is involved, no individual or group within an organization should act alone. The business managers must decide when the risks are great and the answers unclear.

The management of a records and information management program affects the entire organization. If records are not effectively created, they will not be admissible in evidence nor acceptable by regulatory agencies. If records are not kept long enough, the company may be subject to fines, penalties and other loss of rights. If records are kept too long, the organization could experience adverse consequences in litigation. If records are not properly microfilmed or maintained in computer form, the company's valuable information may be lost and its ability to function compromised. The impact of a bad decision related to information could be catastrophic for the welfare of the organization.

When the law is precise and the legal requirements known, the organization should carefully follow those requirements without much discussion. In the area of legal considerations for records and information management programs, the course of action is often not clear. Since so much risk is involved and the welfare of the organization in question, the business managers have both the right and the responsibility to make the ultimate decision regarding the company's valuable records and information.

See Chapter 6 for details regarding the Legal Group File.

To facilitate this review, the various legal issues must be compiled and analyzed in the Legal Group File. In some organizations this may initially be performed by the records manager with subsequent review by the legal department; in others, the legal department will initiate these activities. Each issue related to the legal consideration must be identified and a risk level determined.

Records Retention Procedures

Risk Versus Cost

When deciding among the risk of various options, the lowest risk alternative may not always be the best for the organization. In many cases, the alternative with the lowest risk is often the most costly to implement. For example, in order to ensure the preservation of certain records required by law, some organizations will initiate a microfilm program. While microfilm may often be the best alternative for protecting information, the cost may be unjustifiably high especially for records which only need to be maintained for a short period of time, such as three years. While the law may require the organization to keep a record for the three year period, it does not mandate extraordinary and costly measures to ensure their preservation under all circumstances such as a natural disaster.

Business managers must weigh the cost of the "low risk" solution versus the cost of the "high risk" solution, especially when compared to the cost to the organization if disaster strikes. What is the cost of microfilming records required to be kept for only three years versus the cost to the organization if those records were inadvertently destroyed or lost prior to the end of the three-year period? A low or no-risk solution is often very costly now. However, a high-risk solution may cost nothing now but may be very costly later.

The risk versus the cost must therefore be carefully weighed in order to determine the most appropriate solution for an organization. Generally, an organization should accept a reasonable amount of legal risk and incur a reasonable amount of cost to keep the risk at that reasonable level.

Probability of Adverse Consequences

When determining risk, it is also appropriate to determine the likelihood of adverse consequences. In some cases, although the penalty may be high for certain legal actions, the probability may be low in terms of actually being in that situation.

A statute of limitations, for example, is not a legal requirement for keeping records. It merely states a period of time during which an organization may or may not want to maintain records. Although the decision to maintain records may often depend upon the operational needs of the organization for those records, the decision may also involve legal considerations related to litigation. The organization may need those records to pursue its case or defend itself in a lawsuit.

In determining the records retention period for contract records covered by a statute of limitation, the organization must therefore undertake a risk assessment to determine the risks of having or not having those records, the cost of maintaining them or not, and the probability of certain key events occurring. Only through analysis, can the business managers determine which alternative reflects the best interests of the organization.

Risk Assessment: An Example

When analyzing legal considerations related to records and information, three major components of risk assessment must all be considered:

- *Risk*: The type of harm that may result from an action.

- *Cost*: The cost of this harm and the cost of preventing the harm.

- *Probability*: The likelihood that the harm will occur.

The interaction of these three components can be clearly seen in the following fact situation:

ABC Company is a large company performing contract work for others. It operates in states which have a six-year statute of limitations covering breach of contract. After an extensive analysis of prior lawsuits against the company or against other companies in the industry, it has been determined that the company's records are generally helpful to the organization during the first three years after the termination of the contract and generally harmful during the last three years. The harm generally results from smaller companies undertaking nuisance suits (without merit) in hope of a quick settlement. During these nuisance suits, ABC Company's records are often subpoenaed by the other party to either force a settlement or perhaps to embellish their claims.

Industry analysis has also indicated that the availability of company records allowed the company to defend itself in 30 percent of these cases but also resulted in losing about 70 percent or forcing a settlement to reduce costs to the company. The total amount of potential claims facing the company during years four through six after the typical contracts terminate was estimated at $5 million, plus $1 million in staff time to store and retrieve these records.

The total amount of risk facing the organization can be viewed as the potential loss of $5 million. If the company ended up losing all these lawsuits, that would be the total amount the company might be forced to pay to others. By destroying records three years after a contract terminates, the company would probably save $3.5 million (for potential losses in 70 percent of the cases) but risk $1.5 million (for potential wins in 30 percent of the cases). An additional $1 million in storage costs and staff time will be saved either way. It is therefore determined that since the risk to the company is greater for keeping the records than for destroying them, it would cost the company less by destroying records three years after the contract ends. The company also incurs some risk by even making the above determination. While records can legally be destroyed during the statute of limitations period, some may view this decision as a deliberate attempt to obstruct justice or to disadvantage potential litigants. Since all contract records will be consistently destroyed three years after the contracts terminate, rather than destroyed selectively, the risk is small that a judge would reach such a harsh conclusion. The probability is also small that this issue will even be raised.

The risk assessment reviewed the potential harm to the organization, the cost of the various alternatives, and the probability of the alternatives occurring. These are clearly business decisions for business managers to review. The legal considerations are reflected only in determining the risk facing the organization.

Glossary

Active record. A record that is regularly referenced or required for current use.

Adverse inference. A finding by a court in litigation that information contained in documents or other evidence, inappropriately destroyed by a party, is unfavorable to that party, even though the full content of the records or evidence was never reviewed by the court.

Audit. A periodic examination of an organization to determine whether appropriate procedures and practices are followed. See also *tax audit* and *tax hold*.

Business organization. The structure or form of a business such as corporation, partnership, limited partnership, or sole proprietorship.

Capital gain or loss. A tax term indicating the amount of gain or loss realized when the purchase price plus cost of improvements is deducted from the ultimate sale price of capital property.

Capital property. A form of property designed to be used or kept for long periods of time, including real property, buildings, equipment and investments.

Contract. An agreement between two or more people that creates, modifies, or destroys their legal relationship through a promise made by one party and assented to by the other.

Corporation. A legal entity created by authority of state law that grants a group of people certain legal powers, rights, privileges, and liabilities, distinct from those of the individuals making up the group.

Depreciation. The loss in value of property or equipment used over time for business purposes and which is the amount that can be deducted on a tax return for this purpose.

Destruction, suspension of. A term used in record retention programs to indicate the process or procedure implemented to stop the destruction of records when it has been determined that litigation, government investigation or audit is pending or imminent.

Doing business. The acts of an organization which place it under the jurisdiction or control of government, courts, or law.

Duplicate. A facsimile or replica "produced by the same impression as the original or from the same matrix as the original by means of photography, including enlargements and miniatures, or by mechanical or electronic re-recording, chemical reproduction, or other equivalent techniques which accurately reproduces the original." (Uniform Rules of Evidence)

Employment actions. Decisions and actions by employers that affect employees in areas such as promotion, demotion, transfer, selection for training, layoffs, or recalls.

Hazardous substance. A material or chemical determined to be harmful to human health.

Hold. A term used in record retention schedules to indicate that certain records cannot be destroyed even though the record retention period has concluded. See also *tax hold* and *legal hold.*

Inactive records. Records still needed by an organization but not for current operations.

Indefinite. A term used in records retention schedules to indicate that the retention period for certain records cannot be determined in advance and that these records must be reviewed periodically to determine whether they can be destroyed.

Law. An obligation to act or not act legitimately imposed by statute, rule or regulation, local ordinance or resolution, or judicial decision.

Lawsuit. Same as *Litigation*.

Legal compliance. The process or procedure to ensure that the organization is following relevant laws.

Legal consideration. Information related to a law or legal action that has a bearing on the records retention period but which is not a legal requirement to act or not act.

Legal group file. A summary of legal requirements and legal considerations, in a simplified form, for use in a records retention schedule.

Legal hold. A term used in records retention programs to indicate that certain records cannot yet be destroyed, even if otherwise permitted by the records retention schedule, because they are subject to litigation or government investigation.

Legal requirements. The obligation under a law to act or not act in the specified manner.

Legal research. The process of identifying and locating legal requirements.

Legal research index. An index prepared during legal research for a records retention program to organize the relevant laws.

Limitation of action. See *Statute of limitations*.

Limitation of assessment. The period of time after a tax return is filed or the tax becomes due during which the government tax agency can determine or modify the amount of taxes owed.

Limited partnership. A special form of partnership consisting of general partners who operate the partnership and are liable for any debts or losses, and limited partners who contribute capital and share in profits, but are not liable for debts or losses of the partnership beyond the amount contributed.

Litigation. A proceeding in a court of law to enforce a right. Same as *lawsuit*.

Litigation protection. The process or procedures followed, in accordance with laws, that places an organization in the best possible position in litigation.

Obstruction of justice. A deliberate act designed to interfere with a government investigation or judicial proceeding.

Office of record. The group, department, or office in an organization responsible for maintaining the official records for the total records retention period.

One-time project. A project, such as the destruction or microfilming of records, conducted in a non-recurring manner.

Original. The "writing or recording itself or any counterpart intended to have the same effect by a person executing or issuing it. If data are stored in a computer or similar device, any printout or other output readable by sight, shown to reflect the data accurately, is an *original*." (Uniform Rules of Evidence).

Partnership. An association of people working together and sharing profits.

Pending. The action or activity is in progress but not yet completed.

Permanent. The continued preservation of information or other matter forever, without any limit in time. A term sometimes used in laws to mean *durable* rather than *forever*.

Personal records. Same as *private records.*

Private records. Records belonging to an individual that have no content relevant to the organization or were not produced using resources of the organization. Same as *personal records.*

Product liability. The legal responsibility of a manufacturer or seller to the purchaser or consumer of the product for the design, safety, and utility of the product.

Record. The act of preserving information on any media that can be retrieved at a later time. "Letters, words, sounds, or numbers, or their equivalent, set down by handwriting, typewriting, printing, photostating, photographing, magnetic impulse, mechanical electronic recording, or other form of data compilation", including "still photographs, X–rays, X-ray films, video tapes, and motion pictures." (Uniform Rules of Evidence)

Record series. A group of similar or related records, used or filed as a unit.

Record value. The importance or usefulness of a record for operational, legal, fiscal, historical or other purpose.

Recordkeeping requirements. The obligations of law related to the creation, maintenance and disposition of records.

Records destruction. The process of totally obliterating information on records by any method to make the information unreadable or unusable under any circumstances.

Records management. The systematic control of all records from creation or receipt through processing, distribution, maintenance and retrieval, to their ultimate disposition.

Records manager. An individual, knowledgeable in records managements, designated by an organization to control the records management program.

Records retention period. The period of time during which records must be maintained by an organization because they are needed for operational, legal, fiscal, historical or other purposes. Records should be destroyed after the termination of the retention period.

Records retention program. A component of the total records management program that determines the period of time for retaining records and controls the ultimate disposition of records at the appropriate time.

Records retention schedule. A document prepared as part of a records retention program that lists the period of time for retaining records.

Regulation. A law prepared by a regulatory agency acting under authority granted by Congress or the state legislature.

Regulatory agency. A government entity authorized to issue laws in the form of rules or regulations, conduct investigations or quasi judicial hearings, or initiate enforcement proceedings for existing laws.

Statute. A law prepared by the United States Congress or a state legislature.

Statute of limitations. A time period after an event during which a legal action or lawsuit may be initiated.

Systematic. The process of conducting activities or procedures conducted according to a system, method, or plan in a regular, orderly or methodical manner.

Tax audit. The review by a government tax agency of tax returns and tax records to determine whether the correct amount of tax was paid.

Tax hold. A term used in records retention schedules to indicate that certain records cannot yet be destroyed, even when otherwise permitted under the records retention program, because they are currently subject to audit or the audit period for those records has been extended.

Other Publications and Services . . .

Recordkeeping Requirements

Legally, how long must you keep tax returns? How soon can you destroy old employment records? How many hours would it take you to track down the hundreds of applicable federal and state laws? How many documents are needlessly, expensively stored because no one know the answers?

Recordkeeping Requirements gives the answers, saves time, and free up valuable space by identifying in clear, simple language, what the laws say and how to comply. The only book of its kind, this 344-page book *is a guide to what you have to keep and what you can — and perhaps should — destroy.*

Provides quick answers: What are your legal responsibilities? What laws affect your records, and how do you apply them?

Provides detailed analysis: How to analyze the six types of records retention laws that affect your records. How to apply the laws to your records.

Avoids confusing legal jargon: Written in straightforward and non-technical style for those with little or no recordkeeping experience (yet is sufficiently detailed for those who need in-depth, accurate information).

Provides exact language of the most needed laws: Includes state and federal laws for tax, employment, contracts, etc.

Legal Requirements for Business Records

For those who need all the information, *Legal Requirements for Business Records* gives the full text of over 7,500 United States federal and state laws that affect recordkeeping. Our annual update service helps you comply with the new laws!

Legal Requirement for Microfilm, Comuter and Optical Disk Records: Evidence, Regulation, Government and International Requirements

When an organization develops an advanced records system utilizing technologies such as microfilm, computer and optical disk, legal question can be expected. Will courts permit their use? Can the original recors be destroyed aftery they have been reproduced? When a regulation speicifies the tcreation of particular records, must a particular for the the records be used?

This 500-page book provides you:
☐ Detailed legal analysis and recommendations.
☐ Full text of major United States federal and state laws and international laws .
☐ Text of Uniform Laws and Guidelines.
☐ Annual supplements to keep you informed.

Law, Records and Information Management: The Court Cases

Compliance with statutes and regulations is not enough. The courts interpret these laws and expect you to have a system in place to identify and retrieve records when presented with a subpoena in litigation.

This 600-page book provides you:
☐ Selected text from over 200 leading court cases.
☐ Detailed legal analysis of the important cases.
☐ Indexes, tables and cross reference to help you find relevant informaltion.
☐ Practical, procedural recommendations.
☐ Annual supplements to keep you informed.

Retention!

Our new software package gives you *The Skupsky Retention Method* in computer form. We also provide you with the basic data to help you develop a records retention schedule quickly and accurately, plus the text of the records retention laws in computer-readable form taken from *Legal Requirements for Business Records*.

Order Form

Please complete and send to: **Information Requirements Clearinghouse**
5600 South Quebec Street, Suite 250C
Englewood, Colorado 80111
(303) 721-7500,   FAX (303) 721-8849

Please complete this form to order additional books or request information.

Name _____ Title _____
Company _____
Address _____
City _____ State _____ Zip Code _____
Phone (   ) _____

Orders

Number	Description	Price	Total
	Law, Records and Information Management: The Court Cases	$ 95.00	
	Legal Requirements for Microfilm, Computer and Optical Disk Records	$ 59.00	
	Records Retention Procedures	$ 39.00	
	Recordkeeping Requirements	$ 25.00	
	Subtotal		
	Tax (Colorado residents add sales tax)		
	*Shipping and Handling: $4.50 for first book, plus $2.00 for each additional book		$ 4.50 $
	Total		

☐ Enclosed is $ _____ check or money order for payment in full.

☐ Charge to: ___ MasterCard ___ Visa   Date card expires: _____

Credit Card Number: ☐☐☐☐☐☐☐☐☐☐☐☐☐☐☐☐

Signature of card holder _____

☐ Send me information about your records retention software, **Retention!.**
☐ Send me information about your seminars and consulting services.

*International Orders

Canada: Add $10.00 additional shipping and handing.
Other: Add $25.00 additional shipping and handling.

GUARANTEE: If you are dissatisfied with our publication for any reason, please return it in resalable condition with proof of purchase within 30 days of receipt. Information Requirements Clearinghouse will promptly refund your purchase price.